# HOME BAKING

# BISCUITS
# & COOKIES

# HOME BAKING

# BISCUITS
# & COOKIES

## Wendy Hobson

AURA

This edition published in 2013
by Baker & Taylor (UK) Limited,
Bicester, Oxfordshire

Copyright © 2013 Arcturus Publishing Limited
26/27 Bickels Yard, 151–153 Bermondsey Street
London SE1 3HA

ISBN: 978-1-90940-943-9
AD002703EN

Printed in China

# Contents

✳ ✳ ✳ ✳ ✳ ✳ ✳ ✳

# Introduction

✳ ✳ ✳ ✳ ✳ ✳ ✳

In recent years, most of us haven't bothered to bake our own biscuits and cookies – it's so easy to pick up a packet from the huge range on the shelves. But now, baking is back!

Making biscuits and cookies is not difficult – it's just that we have largely lost the inclination to do so. It is much quicker to buy them, and we have become far too accustomed to the uniformity of biscuits extruded from a machine, each one perfect and perfectly indistinguishable from its neighbour. How dull!

There are so many reasons why it is great to make your own biscuits and cookies, and the recipes in this book will convince you of that – but before you start cooking, here are some of them.

✳   It is really easy to make all kinds of biscuits and cookies, plain and fancy, sweet and savoury. There are no fancy techniques in this book. It is filled with interesting, tasty and easy-to-follow recipes that family and friends will enjoy.

❋ Most are very quick both to make and to bake, so there's no waiting around. In fact, it's probably quicker than going to the shops to buy a packet.

❋ Baking biscuits is great fun for kids, and it's a good way to introduce them to a healthy interest in food and cooking.

❋ You don't need any special equipment. Just your usual baking things will do fine – a bowl, a spoon, a rolling pin. What you don't have, you can improvise.

❋ Every biscuit is different. You'll love those idiosyncrasies that set home-baked apart from mass-produced.

❋ You can fill them with all your favourite ingredients, adapting recipes to make your perfect biscuit.

❋ The recipes don't include any obscure and hard-to-find ingredients, so there will be no need to search online sources before you can make a particular biscuit.

✻ There are no additives or preservatives to worry about, no E numbers creeping into your food that you don't want or need.

✻ You will know exactly what goes into your biscuits and cookies, so they will be ideal for people with food allergies or intolerances. There's even a special section of gluten-free recipes at the end of the book.

✻ The instructions are all given step by step so you will know exactly what you are to do, whether you are an experienced baker or a beginner.

✻ Biscuits make great gifts for birthdays, for a hostess, or just as a little thank you.

✻ And did I mention that they taste delicious? A clear case of last but not least.

If that doesn't convince you to get out your baking things and bake biscuits, you could be a lost cause – but since you chose to pick up this book and read it so far, the odds are that you are now raring to go!

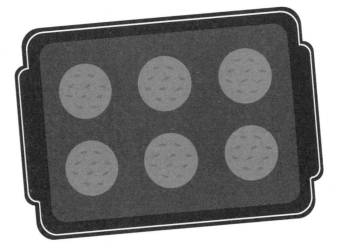

# CHAPTER 1

✳✳✳✳✳✳✳✳

# GETTING STARTED

It's said that the difference between a biscuit and a cake is that a biscuit is crisp and goes soft when it is stale, while a cake does the opposite. But where do biscuits stop and cookies begin? I don't think we need to argue too much about definitions as long as we have a selection of delicious goodies to enjoy with our cup of tea or coffee.

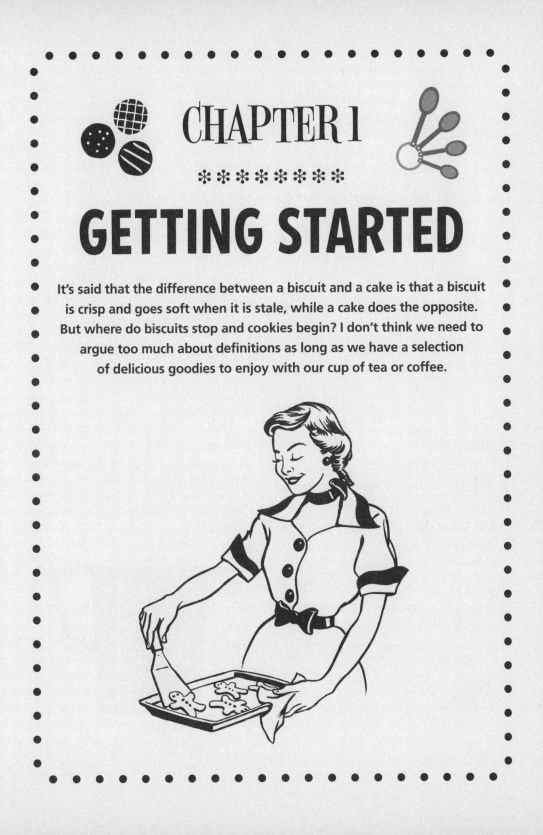

# Equipment

❊ ❊ ❊ ❊ ❊ ❊ ❊

*The great thing about making biscuits and cookies is that you really don't need any special equipment, especially as this is a collection of traditional family biscuits rather than a complex selection for serious bakers.*

Don't dash out to the shops to stock up on fancy gadgets or equipment you are not sure you will ever use – just start with what you already have in the kitchen and improvise when you need to, then you'll soon work out what you need to add to your battery of equipment.

When you do decide what you would like to buy, you'll find plenty of choice in your local kitchen shop, hardware store or supermarket.

## MEASURING

The accurate measuring of your ingredients is an important first step to success.

**Kitchen scales** Choose scales that are accurate, easy to clean and calibrated so you can use metric or imperial measurements; most are now electronic and the settings can be changed at the touch of a button.

**Measuring jugs** A Pyrex measuring jug is very handy as it can also be used for heating ingredients in the microwave. Some measuring jugs have the calibration on the inside so that you can see the figures more easily while you pour in the liquid – look out for them, as they are very convenient.

**Measuring spoons** A set of measuring spoons is far more reliable to use than your ordinary cutlery. When measuring 1 tsp or 1 tbsp, fill the spoon, then flatten the top with a knife to get the correct measure.

**Cup measures** You may have recipe books, or find recipes on the internet, in which the ingredients are given in cups. These are based on volume, not weight. The easiest way to use these recipes is to buy a set of cup measures. For liquid, 1 cup = 250ml/8fl oz. For other ingredients, you need to fill the cup and level the top for each, since volume to weight ratios differ – for example, 1 cup of flour weighs about 100g/4oz, whereas 1 cup caster sugar weighs around 225g/8oz and icing sugar 125g/4½oz.

> **VALUE AND QUALITY**
> If you really take to baking, it is best to buy a few good-quality items and add to your equipment gradually. They will be better value and you'll get better results than you would from buying cheaply.

## MIXING AND SHAPING

All you really need is a couple of bowls and spoons, though acquiring a few other utensils will speed things along.

**Bowls** A large mixing bowl is a must. A Pyrex bowl is useful, as you can see if you have mixed all the ingredients, but my favourite is a melamine bowl with a handle on one side and a lip on the other – it looks like a cross between a giant's teacup and a jug. It's easier to hold, lighter, and more accurate when transferring ingredients.

A few smaller bowls are also useful for mixing separate ingredients – glass pudding basins come in handy sizes. When whisking, you need a wide bowl that allows you to whisk the air into the mix.

**Mixers and processors** A little electric hand whisk is a useful tool as it can be used for beating and whisking, the beaters are easy to wash, and it doesn't take much space in the cupboard. It replaces a lot of elbow grease. Of course, you can also use your food processor, especially for all-in-one mixes and for chopping.

**Spoons and other utensils** A couple of wooden spoons are good for mixing, plus large metal spoons for folding. A little hand whisk is useful for whisking, and a flexible scraper is handy for getting the last of the mixture out of the bowl.

The most commonly used biscuit cutters are 7.5cm/3in, 5cm/2in and 3cm/1¼in round, either fluted or smooth-edged. If you don't have any, you can use a cup or a mug and run round the edge with a knife. Square or rectangular cutters are ideal for those biscuits that we traditionally bake in those shapes, such as custard creams. However, there are biscuit cutters in pretty much any size and shape, and it's up to you which type of biscuits you use them for!

A flat, wide spatula is the best thing for lifting baked biscuits from the baking sheet to the cooling rack when the biscuits are still warm and slightly soft.

You may need a piping bag for some biscuits and cookies, but you can always use a plastic bag instead (see page 42), so there is no need to delay trying a recipe until you have bought one.

**Rolling out** Ideally, use a rolling pin, but if you don't have one, just fill a smooth water bottle with cold water, making sure it's tightly sealed. The water will provide the necessary weight and will also keep the dough cool. An empty glass milk bottle will also suffice.

## BAKING

Here are your few essentials for baking.

**Baking sheets** For biscuits, you'll need one or two good-quality baking sheets.

**Lining papers** Flexible silicone baking sheet liners are efficient and washable. If you use those, or a good-quality non-stick baking sheet, you should not need lining papers. If your biscuits tend to stick, grease the baking sheet, then cover it with paper (or 'parchment'). The grease will hold the paper in place.

For some cookies, you will also need edible rice paper. It sticks to the cookie and you just tear away the excess paper and leave the rest.

**Cooling rack** This helps biscuits and cookies to cool quickly as the air can circulate on all sides.

# Ingredients

*All the biscuits in this book are made with readily available ingredients so that they are straightforward to cook in a home kitchen. You should find everything you need on the baking shelves in the supermarket.*

The starting point for most recipes is a combination of flour, butter and sugar. However, there are many permutations of even those three ingredients, given all the different flours, fats, sugars and other sweeteners such as honey and syrup that are available.

## FLOURS

Most of the biscuits in this book are made with plain flour, although some use wholemeal flour. This gives a denser result, so it is more suitable for crunchy, thick biscuits. Half plain flour and half wholemeal gives good results.

You can also use cornflour, gram flour, rice flour, buckwheat flour or potato flour, and these come into their own when you want to make gluten-free biscuits. You can also buy special gluten-free plain flour, which is a mix of various suitable flours. Another option is to use ground nuts for all or part of the dry ingredients for biscuits, bringing in a whole new range of flavours.

Some biscuits – those on the cookie/cake borderline – need a raising agent, so these may use baking powder, bicarbonate of soda and cream of tartar. Again, there are gluten-free versions.

## FATS AND OILS

Butter is listed in most of the recipes; I use unsalted butter. You can use a spread instead, as long as it is suitable for baking – check the label. Some biscuits and cookies use oil to moisten the batter mixture.

## SWEET THINGS

Sugar comes in many variations, of course: caster, golden caster, granulated, dark and light soft brown, crunchy demerara, icing. If in doubt, caster sugar is most often used for biscuits and cookies as it is a uniformly fine sugar.

You can also sweeten biscuits with honey, syrup, treacle or agave syrup – all will give a slightly different flavour. I also use canned caramel – you'll find it in the supermarket with condensed milk. Sweet fruits will flavour your biscuits, too.

## EGGS

Unlike cakes, not all biscuits use eggs, although some do. I generally use medium free-range eggs. If you use small or large eggs, remember that you may need to add a little more liquid, usually milk, or a little more flour to make sure the mixture is the right consistency.

You often need to beat or mix biscuit dough to blend the ingredients properly to a malleable dough. If you think the mixture is not going to form a dough, give it time and keep mixing rather than adding more liquid immediately.

## OTHER INGREDIENTS

Many biscuits contain chunky nuts of all kinds, from almonds to pecans and pistachios. Dried fruits are also a tasty inclusion, from the currants in garibaldi biscuits to raisins, apricots and even mango. Throw in chocolate chips, glacé cherries and oats and you have yet more variety.

Finally, try spicing up your biscuits with a hot touch of ginger or warming allspice or cinnamon.

# Basic Methods

✳ ✳ ✳ ✳ ✳ ✳ ✳ ✳

*All the recipes give you step-by-step instructions, but if you are new to baking, take time to read this little introduction to baking techniques.*

## FOR BEGINNERS

Here are a few guidelines for beginners so you start off on the right foot. If you have baked a few biscuits and cookies already, you can skip over this section.

**Preparation** The first step when you want to do some baking is to decide what you are going to make before you go shopping. That sounds blindingly obvious, but it's really annoying to come home from the supermarket and decide to make some custard creams, only to discover that you haven't any custard.

Obviously, you should wash your hands and make sure your kitchen surfaces are clean; basic hygiene applies whatever you are doing in the kitchen. An apron is a good idea, too.

Read through the recipe so that it doesn't hold any surprises. Gather the ingredients in a convenient place, making sure you still have enough working room, especially if you are rolling out dough on the worktop. Get your baking sheets ready, along with utensils, baking paper, or whatever else you are going to need.

Now turn on the oven to the recommended temperature so it can heat up, ready for the biscuits to go in. The exception here, of course, is if you are going to chill a dough before you bake it, in which case, leave this step until indicated in the recipe.

**Measuring and mixing** Now measure out your ingredients. If the individual ingredients are going to be mixed, they can go in the same bowl. Most scales allow you to return to zero before you add the next ingredient, so there's no excuse if your maths is not too good!

Next, mix the ingredients. This may involve melting, beating or whisking. Sometimes biscuit doughs take a little effort to work to a pliable dough because if they are too moist, they run all over the baking sheet when you put them in the oven. Mix really thoroughly before you start adding more liquid. You'll soon get used to it. Be patient!

**Getting ready for the oven** Some biscuits are dropped in spoonfuls onto your baking sheet. Make sure you allow plenty of space between the biscuits as they are likely to spread once they go into the oven.

If you have a very firm dough, you may shape it into balls and flatten them on to the baking sheet, or roll it out and cut into shapes with a biscuit cutter. Biscuits made with these firmer doughs do not spread when cooking, so you can place them quite close together on the baking sheets.

**Baking** Always set a timer when you put a batch of biscuits in the oven; as they take such a short time to cook, it is easy to become distracted and not realize that 10 minutes or so has already passed. Since ovens vary, set your timer for less than the recommended time at first. If the biscuits are ready – golden brown and slightly darker around the edges – before the specified time, take them out. Recipes can only ever be a guide, and you need to adapt them to suit how your oven works. You can always leave the biscuits in for longer, but once they are overcooked, there's not much you can do with them.

**The final stage** While your biscuits are cooking, you have just enough time to tidy away the ingredients and wash up or load the dishwasher. The boring bit – which no-one enjoys! – can be lightened by the fact that you can lick the spoon before you wash up and tidy up. It's much better to clean up now, while you can enjoy the smell of the biscuits or cookies in the oven.

When your biscuits are ready, leave them on the baking tray for a minute or two. This allows them to harden slightly as they cool. If you try to move them when they are just out of the oven, they will be too soft and therefore likely to crumble. After a couple of minutes, they will be easier to lift off the baking sheet using a wide slice and pop on the cooling rack to cool and harden.

## MAKING MISTAKES

Don't be discouraged if some of your biscuits aren't absolutely perfect – part of the charm of home-made biscuits is the fact that they are not uniform. If this means some odd shapes or different sizes, who cares? If they taste good, they are good. Next time you make them, you'll improve.

## SEPARATING EGGS

To separate the white from the yolk, have two bowls ready. Crack the egg, then tip the yolk into one half of the shell, allowing the white to drop into one of the bowls. Tip the yolk into the other half of the shell, and repeat until the egg white has all dropped away. Put the yolk in the other bowl.

## WHISKING

The point of whisking is to introduce as much air as possible into the mixture, so use a wide bowl and a hand or electric whisk, or a food processor. With a hand whisk, use a wide circular motion, lifting it out of the mixture as you work.

**Whisking egg whites** Always use a clean, grease-free bowl and whisk or the whites won't fluff up. They should go frothy and increase in volume until they form soft peaks when you lift out the whisk. Once that happens, stop whisking and go on to the next stage.

If you are adding sugar, do so gradually, whisking all the time until the mixture is glossy. If you pour sugar in one go onto whisked egg whites, you'll just flatten them.

**Whipping cream** Use the same technique to whip double or whipping cream until it is thick and stands in peaks when you lift out the whisk. Don't overbeat or it will start to separate.

## BEATING

This is just vigorous mixing of ingredients, with a hand whisk, a wooden spoon or your food processor. Biscuit doughs, being dryer and firmer than cakes, are sometimes quite hard to beat. You might think at first that there is not enough liquid or fat to bind the dry ingredients, but just keep mixing and you will find that they come together after a while. Start with a spoon or your processor, and finish drawing the dough together by hand.

**Beating eggs and sugar** You often beat together eggs and sugar at the start of a recipe. Use an electric mixer, if you have one, and beat until the mixture goes pale and light, and trails off the whisk in ribbons when you lift it out of the bowl.

## FOLDING

When adding light ingredients such as egg whites to a mixture, first add a small quantity of the egg white to make the mixture lighter and looser. Then add the rest, cut through the middle of the mixture with a metal spoon and fold the spoon round the edge so the ingredients are mixed together gently.

## RUBBING IN

This is the technique of mixing butter into flour. Lift small amounts of the mixture and rub it through your fingertips until the mixture resembles coarse breadcrumbs. Alternatively, you can use a pastry blender, or pulse in the food processor.

## MELTING

Quite a few biscuit mixes start with melted ingredients, particularly butter and chocolate.

**Butter** Melt gently in a heavy-based pan over a very low heat, stirring frequently. Remove from the heat before all the butter has melted and keep stirring as the remaining solid butter will melt in the heat of the mixture.

**Chocolate** Always melt chocolate very gently or it will go grainy and spoil; there's not much you can do to rectify that. Place a heatproof bowl over a pan of gently simmering water, making sure the water is not touching the bowl. Break the chocolate into the bowl and stir occasionally until it is almost melted. Remove the bowl from the pan and continue to stir until it has all melted.

## ROLLING AND CUTTING OUT

Always roll out on a work surface lightly dusted with flour, otherwise the biscuit dough will stick and tear. Dip your hand into the flour and rub your hand along your rolling pin, too, to make sure that doesn't stick either. Roll away from you, lift and turn the dough, then roll again. If you find the dough difficult to handle, take half the dough at a time so you are dealing with a smaller piece.

Cut out your biscuits using a biscuit cutter, keeping them as close as possible to each other, and transfer to the baking sheet using a flat slice. Then you can reroll the dough and cut another batch, continuing until you have used all the dough.

## LINING BAKING SHEETS

Silicone baking sheet liners will save you a lot of time and effort. If you don't want to buy them and you find that your biscuits stick to the baking sheet, line it with baking paper so that you can lift your biscuits off easily without them sticking and spoiling.

### SPACING BISCUITS

When you put biscuit dough on a baking sheet to cook, some will spread a lot, some not at all. As a rule of thumb, the softer the dough, the further it will spread. Generally speaking, rolled biscuits don't spread.

## HOW DO YOU KNOW THE BISCUITS ARE READY?

You will become more confident with experience, but it is actually quite easy to see when biscuits are ready. If they are thin, they will go golden brown and slightly darker round the edges. Thicker biscuits or cookies will do the same, but may also rise just slightly. Keep a close eye on them through the glass window on the oven door as they will be ready very quickly.

Once you take them out of the oven, they will be very soft. They only go crisp and harden as they cool, so leave them briefly on the baking sheet. You can slide your flat slice under them to make sure they are not stuck, but do it carefully. Once they have had a minute or two to firm up, lift them carefully with a wide, flat spatula or slice and transfer to a wire rack to finish cooling.

## STORAGE AND FREEZING

If you keep your biscuits in an airtight container they will usually stay fresh for several days. They will not last as long in perfect condition as shop-bought biscuits because those contain preservatives, but you gain in so many other ways!

Most of the recipes are suitable for freezing. Cool completely, then wrap in clingfilm and put in a freezer box or bag. Seal, label and freeze for up to a few months. Leave to defrost naturally in the bag for half an hour or so, take them out and separate them, then allow them to finish defrosting. Alternatively, freeze biscuits on a large baking sheet before sealing them in a bag so you can take out one or two biscuits at a time.

Do not freeze no-bake biscuits, biscuits sandwiched with fresh cream or whisked egg white biscuits. These are marked with a ❄ next to the recipe.

Uncooked biscuit dough can be frozen, too. Wrap rolls of it in clingfilm, then a plastic bag, and freeze for up to about a month. You can also pack the rolls in freezer containers, separated by baking parchment. When you want to make biscuits, defrost the rolls, cut off slices and bake according to the recipe.

# Notes on the Recipes

❉ ❉ ❉ ❉ ❉ ❉ ❉ ❉

*Take a look at these notes before you start on the recipes so that you are familiar with the style of the book.*

❋ Eggs, fruit and vegetables are medium unless otherwise stated.

❋ The recipes give metric and imperial measurements. It is advisable to follow just one set of measures in any given recipe.

❋ The ingredients are listed in the order in which they are used.

❋ All spoon measurements are level: 1 tsp = 5ml; 1 tbsp = 15ml.

❋ Wash fresh foods before use.

❋ Can and packet sizes are approximate and will depend on the particular brand.

❋ Taste the food as you cook and adjust seasoning to suit your own taste. Use your discretion in substituting ingredients and personalizing the recipes.

❋ Use whichever kitchen gadgets you like to speed up preparation and cooking times. An electric hand mixer will be the most useful item for both beating and whisking, or you can use a food processor, which is also perfect for grating, slicing, mixing and kneading.

❋ All ovens vary, so regard cooking times as approximate. Keep an eye on the oven while you are baking and adjust cooking times and temperatures to suit your appliance.

❋ I generally recommend a large baking sheet for most recipes but you may find you need two if yours are of a medium size.

## MEASUREMENT CONVERSIONS

If you need to convert your own recipes, you might find these conversions useful. Note that cup measures are based on volume rather than weight, so solid foods do not all have the same ratio of weight to cup. For example, a cup of flour weighs 100g/4oz while a cup of butter weighs 225g/8oz.

### WEIGHT

| Metric | Imperial | Cups |
|--------|----------|------|
| 25–30g | 1oz | |
| 50g | 2oz | |
| 75g | 3oz | |
| 100g | 4oz | 1 cup dried ingredients such as flour |
| 150g | 5oz | |
| 175g | 6oz | 1 cup dried fruit or pulses |
| 200g | 7oz | |
| 225g | 8oz | 1 cup fat or sugar |
| 250g | 9oz | |
| 350g | 12oz | |
| 450g | 1lb | |

## LIQUIDS

| Metric | Imperial | Cups |
|--------|----------|------|
| 5ml | 1 tsp | |
| 15ml | 1 tbsp | |
| 50ml | 2fl oz | ¼ cup |
| 75ml | 2½fl oz | ⅓ cup |
| 120ml | 4fl oz | ½ cup |
| 150ml | 5fl oz | ⅔ cup |
| 175ml | 6fl oz | ¾ cup |
| 250ml | 8fl oz | 1 cup |
| 300ml | 10fl oz | 1¼ cups |
| 450ml | 16fl oz | 2 cups |
| 600ml | 1 pint | 2½ cups |

## LENGTH

| Metric | Imperial |
|--------|----------|
| 2.5cm | 1in |
| 5cm | 2in |
| 10cm | 4in |
| 13cm | 5in |
| 15cm | 6in |
| 20cm | 8in |
| 25cm | 10in |
| 30cm | 12in |
| 35cm | 14in |
| 40cm | 16in |
| 45cm | 18in |

## OVEN TEMPERATURES

| Metric | Imperial | Gas mark | Metric | Imperial | Gas mark |
|--------|----------|----------|--------|----------|----------|
| 110°C | 225°F | gas ¼ | 190°C | 375°F | gas 5 |
| 120°C | 250°F | gas ½ | 200°C | 400°F | gas 6 |
| 140°C | 275°F | gas 1 | 220°C | 425°F | gas 7 |
| 150°C | 300°F | gas 2 | 230°C | 450°F | gas 8 |
| 160°C | 325°F | gas 3 | 240°C | 475°F | gas 9 |
| 180°C | 350°F | gas 4 | | | |

# Troubleshooting

❊ ❊ ❊ ❊ ❊ ❊ ❊ ❊

*No one has a record of 100 per cent success in the kitchen, so be prepared for the odd disaster when you are baking, especially if you are new to it. Here are a few tips to help you avoid problems or find solutions.*

**The mixture is too wet** A very soft mixture will just run all over the baking sheet and won't make good biscuits. Be patient when you are mixing and don't add more liquid unless you are absolutely sure it is necessary.

**Don't set the oven too high** Most biscuits are cooked at 180°C/350°F/gas 4 or sometimes at 200°C/400°F/gas 6 – rarely hotter.

**The biscuits have all run together** Your mixture was too wet. Use a pizza wheel to trim the edges, then cut them into neat shapes while they are still warm. Cool slightly on the baking sheet, then transfer to a wire rack to finish cooling.

**The edges are burnt** You cooked the biscuits for too long. The edges are likely to be darker than the rest of the biscuit but if they are burnt the flavour of the biscuits will be spoilt. You may be able to cut off the edges while they are still warm, using a sharp knife.

**The biscuits broke when transferred to the cooling rack** You tried to lift them before they had begun to cool and harden. If they have crumbled, then complete the process – crumble all of them and serve sprinkled on ice-cream.

**The biscuits are burnt** Perhaps the oven was too hot, or they have been baked too long. If the flavour is affected there's not much you can do. Rescue any bits that aren't burnt and mix them into a crumble topping.

**The biscuits have stuck to the tray** There are several reasons for this: perhaps the baking sheet is not very good, you have not greased it sufficiently or a non-stick coating has worn away. While the biscuits are still warm, slide a sharp slice underneath and lift off as much as you can, leaving behind any burnt bits.

# CHAPTER 2

\* \* \* \* \* \* \* \* \*

# TRADITIONAL FAVOURITES

This first section of the recipes includes traditional favourites such as digestives and shortbread. It is a good place to start if you want to get used to the techniques of baking biscuits.

# Crisp, soft & dunkable

❋ ❋ ❋ ❋ ❋ ❋ ❋ ❋

Some of the most traditional and popular biscuits are to be found in this section, from the ubiquitous but still delicious digestive to malted milk biscuit, the nursery favourite.

For most of us, one particular type of biscuit has a special place in our memory. Perhaps our grandmothers used to serve them, or we remember them from school. Maybe we had dunking contests with friends, always ending up with a mush of collapsed biscuit in the bottom of the cup!

You may be used to treating yourself to a packet of your 'memory biscuits' every now and then, but how much more fun it would be to be able to make them! It's much easier than you think, and it also takes very little time. The fact that the biscuits won't be perfectly round and uniform is an advantage, because your guests will know you have gone to the extra trouble of making something just for them – which is quite a compliment. That is, of course, if you decide to share them!

# Digestive Biscuits

*Voted in the popular press as Britain's favourite biscuit, digestives account for one in nine of all the commercially made biscuits we buy.*

**INGREDIENTS** *Makes 12 biscuits*

50g/2oz wholemeal flour
50g/2oz plain flour, plus extra for dusting
100g/4oz medium oatmeal
30g/1oz caster sugar
¼ tsp bicarbonate of soda
100g/4oz butter
2 tbsp milk (optional)

**METHOD**

**1.** Heat the oven to 200°C/400°F/gas 6 and grease or line a large baking sheet.

**2.** Mix together all the dry ingredients, then rub in the butter until the mixture resembles breadcrumbs. Add the milk a drop at a time, stirring vigorously, until the mixture starts to bind together.

**3.** Using your hands, start to bring all the ingredients into a firm dough and knead gently until smooth.

**4.** Roll out the dough to about 5mm/¼in thick and cut into rounds with a 7.5cm/3in biscuit cutter. Place on the prepared baking sheet.

**5.** Bake in the oven for about 12 minutes until slightly darker around the edges.

**6.** Leave to cool on the baking sheet for 1 minute, then transfer to a wire rack to finish cooling.

# Ginger Biscuits

*Satisfyingly crisp and perfect for dunking, these biscuits contain extra chopped stem ginger to give an interesting texture. If you prefer a slightly stronger ginger flavour, increase the ground ginger to 1 tsp.*

**INGREDIENTS** *Makes 12 biscuits*

50g/2oz plain flour, plus extra for dusting
1 tsp baking powder
½ tsp ground ginger
25g/1oz butter
25g/1oz caster sugar
2 balls of stem ginger, chopped or grated
4 tsp syrup from a jar of stem ginger

**GRATING GINGER**

It is much easier to grate ginger in a small cylinder grater with a handle rather than trying to do it on a square grater.

**METHOD**

**1.** Heat the oven to 180°C/350°F/gas 4 and grease or line a large baking sheet.

**2.** Mix the flour, baking powder and ginger in a bowl. Rub in the butter until the mixture resembles coarse breadcrumbs. Stir in the sugar and ginger, then work to a dough with the ginger syrup.

**3.** Roll out on a lightly floured surface and cut into biscuits with a 7.5cm/3in biscuit cutter. Place them on the prepared baking sheet.

**4.** Bake in the oven for about 10 minutes until slightly darker around the edges.

**5.** Leave to cool on the baking sheet for 1 minute, then transfer to a wire rack to finish cooling.

# Shortbread

✻ ✻ ✻ ✻ ✻ ✻ ✻ ✻

*Shortbread is made of only butter, sugar and flour so use the best ingredients you can for the most delicious results, including a good-quality unsalted butter.*

**INGREDIENTS** *Makes 8 slices*
100g/4oz unsalted butter, softened
50g/2oz caster sugar
225g/8oz plain flour, plus extra
   for dusting

**METHOD**
**1.** Heat the oven to 150°C/300°F/
gas 2 and grease or line a large
baking sheet or a 20cm/8in
shortbread mould or springform
cake tin.
**2.** Beat the butter until it is very soft,
then work in the sugar followed by
the flour until you have a soft dough.
Start with a wooden spoon, then
use your hands. You may have a
spoonful of flour left over, but there
should not be more than that.
**3.** Roll out the mixture on a lightly
floured surface to a 20cm/8in round
or press into the prepared mould

or tin. Prick all over with a fork and
cut through the dough into eight
wedges. This makes it easier to cut
once it has been baked.
**4.** Bake in the oven for 35 minutes
until a pale golden colour.
**5.** Leave to cool in the tin for
2 minutes, then cut through the
markings to make individual
wedges. Leave to cool for another
few minutes before lifting on to a
wire rack to finish cooling.

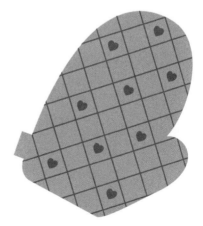

# Shrewsbury Biscuits

*A subtle touch of lemon is the distinctive feature of these light, golden biscuits with their attractive dusting of caster sugar. Use the spare egg whites for Amaretti (page 99) or Hazelnut Macaroons (page 101).*

**INGREDIENTS** *Makes 12 biscuits*

100g/4oz butter
150g/5oz caster sugar
2 egg yolks
225g/8oz plain flour, plus extra for dusting
finely grated zest of 1 lemon
1 tbsp caster sugar

**METHOD**

**1.** Heat the oven to 200°C/400°F/gas 6 and grease or line a large baking sheet.

**2.** Beat together the butter and sugar until pale and creamy. Add the egg yolks a little at a time, beating well. Stir in the flour and lemon zest and mix to a smooth dough.

**3.** Roll out on a lightly floured surface to about 5mm/¼in thick and cut into rounds with a 7.5cm/3in biscuit cutter. Place on the prepared baking sheet.

**4.** Bake in the oven for 10 minutes until pale gold and just browning round the edges.

**5.** Leave to cool on the baking sheet for 1 minute, then transfer to a wire rack and sprinkle with the sugar while still warm. Leave on the rack to finish cooling.

**WILL IT DUNK?**

The idea of dunking a biscuit is that it absorbs as much of the tea as possible before you pop it in your mouth. Opinion varies on the etiquette of dunking, but it is generally considered unsuitable in polite company! The best dunking biscuits are thick and porous, since they can soak up plenty of tea.

# Golden Orange Melts

*These biscuits are ideal for someone on their own because you can make the dough, keep it in the fridge for a week, and simply cut off and bake a few slices each day.*

**INGREDIENTS** *Makes 12 biscuits*

225g/8oz caster sugar
100g/4oz butter
1 egg, lightly beaten
grated zest of 1 orange
300g/11oz plain flour
2 tsp baking powder
2–3 tsp orange juice

## METHOD

**1.** Beat the sugar and butter together until pale and creamy. Beat in the egg and orange zest, then the flour and baking powder with enough orange juice to make a fairly firm dough. Shape into a roll and chill in the fridge overnight.
**2.** Heat the oven to 190°C/375°F/ gas 5 and grease or line a large baking sheet.
**3.** Cut thin slices of dough and arrange on the baking sheet.
**4.** Bake in the oven for 10 minutes until pale golden.
**5.** Leave to cool on the baking sheet for 1 minute, then transfer to a wire rack to finish cooling.

### USING A HALOGEN OVEN

If you have a halogen oven, it is really convenient for cooking biscuits as you can bake small quantities without worrying about wasting fuel. Because cooking times are short, you do need to check frequently until you become used to the length of time it takes for the biscuits to cook and brown. These biscuits take about 6 minutes, but times will vary depending on your oven.

# Raisin Shorts

*Rich shortbread biscuits dotted with raisins, these are slim and simple but tasty, with a sprinkling of sugar on the top. You can substitute demerara sugar for caster sugar, if you prefer.*

**INGREDIENTS** *Makes 12 biscuits*

100g/4oz butter, softened
50g/2oz caster sugar, plus extra for sprinkling
225g/8oz plain flour, plus extra for dusting
100g/4oz raisins

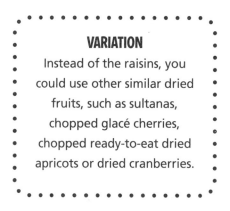

**VARIATION**

Instead of the raisins, you could use other similar dried fruits, such as sultanas, chopped glacé cherries, chopped ready-to-eat dried apricots or dried cranberries.

**METHOD**

**1.** Heat the oven to 150°C/300°F/gas 2 and grease or line a large baking sheet.

**2.** Beat the butter until it is very soft, then work in the sugar followed by the flour and raisins, starting with a wooden spoon, then using your hands.

**3.** Roll out the mixture on a lightly floured surface to about 5mm/¼in thick and cut into rounds with a 7.5cm/3in biscuit cutter. Arrange on the prepared baking sheet and sprinkle with caster sugar.

**4.** Bake in the oven for 20 minutes until a pale golden colour.

**5.** Leave to cool on the baking sheet for 1 minute, then transfer to a wire rack to finish cooling. Serve sprinkled with a little more icing sugar, if liked.

# Malted Milk Biscuits

✳ ✳ ✳ ✳ ✳ ✳ ✳ ✳

*Malted milk biscuits traditionally have a picture of a cow embossed on them, so if you have any biscuit cutters that also mark a pattern on the biscuit, try them out on these.*

**INGREDIENTS** *Makes 12 biscuits*

100g/4oz butter
250g/9oz light brown soft sugar
1 egg, lightly beaten
2 tsp vanilla extract
225g/8oz all-purpose flour,
  plus extra for dusting
1 tsp bicarbonate of soda
a pinch of salt
200g/7oz malted milk powder

**METHOD**

**1.** Heat the oven to 180°C/350°F/ gas 4 and grease or line a large baking sheet.
**2.** Beat the butter and sugar together until pale and creamy. Gradually mix in the egg and vanilla alternately with spoonfuls of the flour, bicarbonate of soda, salt and milk powder and mix to a fairly firm dough.

**3.** Roll out on a lightly floured surface and cut into 12 rectangles with a biscuit cutter. Place on the prepared baking sheet.
**4.** Bake in the oven for 10 minutes until slightly golden brown around the edges.
**5.** Leave to cool on the baking sheet for 1 minute, then transfer to a wire rack to finish cooling.

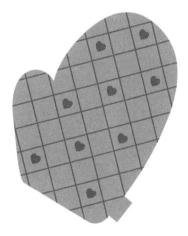

# Nice Biscuits

✳ ✳ ✳ ✳ ✳ ✳ ✳

*In this favourite, old-fashioned biscuit for serving with a cup of tea, the distinctive flavour comes from the coconut and the sprinkle of sugar on the top. Even without 'Nice' written on them, they are easily recognizable.*

**INGREDIENTS** *Makes 12 biscuits*

450g/1lb plain flour, plus extra
    for dusting
40g/1½oz butter
200g/7oz caster sugar, plus extra
    for sprinkling
75g/3oz desiccated coconut
120ml/4fl oz milk
1 tsp vanilla extract
1 tsp bicarbonate of soda

**METHOD**

**1.** Heat the oven to 190°C/375°F/ gas 5 and grease or line a large baking sheet.
**2.** Put the flour in a bowl and rub in the butter until the mixture resembles coarse breadcrumbs. Stir in the sugar and coconut. Gradually add the milk, vanilla and bicarbonate of soda and mix to a fairly stiff dough.

**3.** Roll out the dough on a lightly floured surface and cut into rectangles with a 5×3cm/2×1¼in fluted biscuit cutter. Place on the prepared baking sheet.
**4.** Bake in the oven for about 10 minutes until a light golden brown. Leave to cool on the baking sheet for 1 minute, then transfer to a wire rack, sprinkle with sugar and leave to finish cooling.

# Rich Tea Biscuits

✼ ✼ ✼ ✼ ✼ ✼ ✼ ✼

*You can cut these large and round or make them in finger shapes if you prefer rich tea fingers. Or, of course, you can try something completely different – triangular biscuits make a nice change.*

**INGREDIENTS** *Makes 12 biscuits*
250g/9oz plain flour, plus extra
   for dusting
1 tsp baking powder
a pinch of salt
60g/2½oz vegetable fat
1 egg, lightly beaten
150ml/5fl oz milk

> **NO ROLLING PIN?**
> You can fill a smooth plastic drinks bottle with cold water. The water will not only give it the weight it needs but also keep it cool.

**METHOD**
**1.** Heat the oven to 200°C/400°F/ gas 6 and grease or line a large baking sheet.
**2.** Put the flour, baking powder and salt in a bowl and rub in the fat until the mixture resembles coarse breadcrumbs. Add the egg and enough milk to mix to a soft dough.
**3.** Roll out on a lightly floured surface to about 5mm/¼in thick and cut into 7.5cm/3in rounds with a biscuit cutter. Arrange on the prepared baking sheet.
**4.** Bake in the oven for about 12 minutes until golden brown. Leave to cool on the baking sheet for 1 minute, then transfer to a wire rack to finish cooling.

# Almond Whirls

❋ ❋ ❋ ❋ ❋ ❋ ❋ ❋

*These are light and delicate biscuits with a very airy texture and subtle almond flavour. They look cute topped with a glacé cherry, too. You can increase the almond essence to 1 tsp if you wish.*

## INGREDIENTS *Makes 12 biscuits*

175g/6oz butter
50g/2oz icing sugar, sifted,
    plus extra for dusting
175g/6oz plain flour
½ tsp almond essence
12 glacé cherries

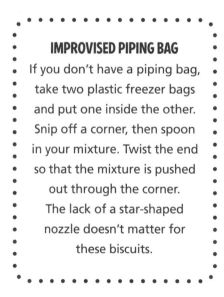

### IMPROVISED PIPING BAG

If you don't have a piping bag, take two plastic freezer bags and put one inside the other. Snip off a corner, then spoon in your mixture. Twist the end so that the mixture is pushed out through the corner. The lack of a star-shaped nozzle doesn't matter for these biscuits.

## METHOD

**1.** Heat the oven to 160°C/325°F/ gas 3 and grease or line a large baking sheet.
**2.** Beat the butter and sugar together until pale and creamy. Beat in the flour and almond essence.
**3.** Spoon the mixture into a piping bag with a star-shaped nozzle and pipe whirls on to the prepared baking sheet. Top each one with a glacé cherry.
**4.** Bake in the oven for 20 minutes until pale golden brown.
**5.** Leave to cool on the baking sheet for 1 minute, then transfer to a wire rack to finish cooling. Dust with icing sugar to serve.

# Golden Crunch

*Deliciously crunchy biscuits with a crackled top, these bake to a golden brown. The hot water will make the bicarbonate of soda bubble to lighten the texture.*

**INGREDIENTS** *Makes 12 biscuits*

100g/4oz self-raising flour, plus extra for dusting
100g/4oz rolled oats
100g/4oz butter
100g/4oz light brown soft sugar
1 tbsp golden syrup
2 tsp bicarbonate of soda
1 tsp boiling water

**METHOD**

**1.** Heat the oven to 180°C/350°F/gas 4 and grease or line a large baking sheet.

**2.** Put the flour and oats in a bowl.

**3.** Gently melt the butter, sugar and syrup in a pan over a low heat, stirring until just melted. Mix the bicarbonate of soda and water, then add to the dry ingredients with the melted mixture. Mix to a soft dough. Roll into balls in lightly floured hands, then press slightly flat and arrange on the prepared baking sheet.

**4.** Bake in the oven for about 15 minutes until golden brown and cracked on the top. Leave to cool on the baking sheet for 1 minute, then transfer to a wire rack to finish cooling.

# Butter Buttons

✳ ✳ ✳ ✳ ✳ ✳ ✳ ✳

*Sweet and buttery, these are easy to make and delicious to eat. Mixing the lemon curd with icing sugar makes it denser and more stable, like an icing, but you could just use lemon curd.*

**INGREDIENTS** *Makes 12 biscuits*

150g/5oz butter

100g/4oz light brown soft sugar

1 egg, lightly beaten

1 tsp vanilla extract

100g/4oz plain flour, plus extra
   for dusting

a pinch of salt

**FOR THE FILLING**

about 90g/3½oz lemon curd

45g/1¾oz icing sugar, sifted

**METHOD**

**1.** Heat the oven to 180°C/350°F/gas 4 and grease or line a large baking sheet.

**2.** Beat the butter and sugar together until pale and creamy. Gradually work in the egg and vanilla alternately with spoonfuls of the flour with the salt added and mix to a soft dough. Shape into a ball, wrap in clingfilm and chill for 30 minutes.

**3.** Using floured hands, shape the mixture into 24 small balls, flatten slightly, and arrange, slightly apart, on the prepared baking sheet.

**4.** Bake in the oven for about 15 minutes until golden brown. Leave to cool on the baking sheet for 1 minute, then transfer to a wire rack to finish cooling.

**5.** Beat the lemon curd with the icing sugar and use to sandwich the biscuits together in pairs.

# Arrowroot Biscuits

✳ ✳ ✳ ✳ ✳ ✳ ✳ ✳

*Arrowroot biscuits were once very popular and should come back into favour. Only slightly sweet, they are also good with cheese.*

**INGREDIENTS** *Makes 12 biscuits*

50g/2oz butter
50g/2oz caster sugar
1 egg, lightly beaten
½ tsp vanilla extract
125g/4½oz plain flour, plus extra
  for dusting
125g/4½oz arrowroot
½ tsp baking powder
a pinch of salt

**METHOD**

**1.** Heat the oven to 180°C/350°F/ gas 4 and grease or line a large baking sheet.
**2.** Beat the butter and sugar together until pale and creamy. Gradually work in the egg and vanilla alternately with spoonfuls of the flour, arrowroot, baking powder and salt and mix to a soft dough.
**3.** Roll out on a lightly floured surface to about 5mm/¼in thick and cut into rounds with a 7.5cm/3in biscuit cutter. Arrange on the prepared baking sheet.
**4.** Bake in the oven for about 8 minutes until golden brown. Leave to cool on the baking sheet for 1 minute, then transfer to a wire rack to finish cooling.

# Plain Cornish Biscuits

✱ ✱ ✱ ✱ ✱ ✱ ✱ ✱

*This is such an easy recipe, ideal for making with children. You can try it with soft brown sugar, if you like, for a slightly different flavour.*

## INGREDIENTS

*Makes 20 small biscuits*

225g/8oz self-raising flour, plus extra
   for dusting
a pinch of salt
100g/4oz butter
175g/6oz caster sugar
1 egg
a little icing sugar, for dusting

## METHOD

**1.** Heat the oven to 200°C/400°F/ gas 6 and grease or line a large baking sheet.
**2.** Put the flour and salt in a bowl and rub in the butter until the mixture resembles coarse breadcrumbs. Stir in the sugar, then mix in the egg and mould to a soft dough.
**3.** Roll out on a lightly floured surface to about 5mm/¼in thick and cut into rounds with a 5cm/2in biscuit cutter. Place the biscuits on the prepared baking sheet.
**4.** Bake in the oven for 10 minutes until golden brown.
**5.** Leave to cool on the baking sheet for 1 minute, then transfer to a wire rack. While the biscuits are still warm, sprinkle with icing sugar through a fine sieve. Leave to finish cooling.

### SPEEDING IT UP

You can use a food processor for any of these recipes to speed up rubbing in, mixing, beating, whisking or blending.

# Cornish Fairings

❋ ❋ ❋ ❋ ❋ ❋ ❋ ❋

*These are traditional melted biscuits made with honey and spices.*
*If you don't have cinnamon or ginger, just use a little more mixed spice.*

## INGREDIENTS *Makes 12 biscuits*

100g/4oz butter
100g/4oz light brown soft sugar
1 tbsp clear honey
175g/6oz plain flour
1 tsp bicarbonate of soda
½ tsp mixed spice
½ tsp ground cinnamon
½ tsp ground ginger

## METHOD

**1.** Heat the oven to 180°C/350°F/ gas 4 and grease two baking sheets.
**2.** Melt the butter, sugar and honey in a pan over a low heat.
**3.** Add the remaining ingredients and beat until well blended. Place spoonfuls well apart on the prepared baking sheets.
**4.** Bake in the oven for about 15 minutes until golden brown and the tops are cracked.
**5.** Leave to cool on the baking sheet for 1 minute, then transfer to a wire rack to finish cooling.

# Coconut Biscuits

✴ ✴ ✴ ✴ ✴ ✴ ✴ ✴

*Crisp and syrupy, these are best rolled into small balls as they spread quite thinly during cooking and will run together if you don't give them enough room.*

**INGREDIENTS** *Makes 20 biscuits*

125g/4½oz butter
100g/4oz caster sugar
50g/2oz golden syrup
100g/4oz plain flour
75g/3oz rolled oats
50g/2oz desiccated coconut
2 tsp bicarbonate of soda
1 tbsp hot water

**METHOD**

**1.** Heat the oven to 160°C/325°F/ gas 3 and grease or line two baking sheets.

**2.** Melt the butter, sugar and syrup over a low heat until dissolved. Stir in the flour, oats and coconut.

**3.** Mix the bicarbonate of soda and hot water, then add to the other ingredients and blend everything together to a fairly stiff mixture. Leave to cool for a minute or so.

**4.** Take heaped teaspoonfuls of the mixture and roll into balls. Place them well apart on the prepared baking sheets.

**5.** Bake in the oven for 20 minutes until golden. Leave to cool on the baking sheet for about 1 minute, then transfer to a wire rack to finish cooling.

# CHAPTER 3

✳✳✳✳✳✳✳✳

# CHOCOLATE BISCUITS

Every now and then, scientists conduct a study on whether or not chocolate makes you feel good. I can't help but think it's a massive waste of time and energy. Most of us know that a little chocolate treat now and then does indeed make us feel good, and a chocolate biscuit fits the bill.

# Making the most of chocolate

✳ ✳ ✳ ✳ ✳ ✳ ✳

There's something relaxing about eating a chocolate biscuit. That must be good for you in itself, as most of us rush around far too much and try to cram more and more into our lives.

It's true, of course, that if the only time we slowed down was for a chocolate biscuit, it wouldn't be a healthy way to live! But given that we know that sweet things in general, and chocolate biscuits in particular, are an occasional treat, they really are worth stopping the clock for. When you make a nice cup of tea – or coffee, or whatever else is your favourite tipple – and sit down for a well-earned break, you can take your time and enjoy the indulgence of a chocolate treat.

In this chapter, you'll find biscuits cooked with chocolate flavourings, chunks of chocolate, or melted chocolate, many of them topped with chocolate coating or icing. There's plain, milk and white, minted and flavoured with orange.

If you can buy the best-quality chocolate, you'll get the finest flavour and a delicious, silky texture. Go for dark chocolate with more than 70 per cent cocoa solids and you won't be disappointed.

It is also important to treat chocolate carefully. If it gets too hot, it will go grainy and then it is ruined, so follow the instructions carefully, especially when melting chocolate (page 18).

# Chocolate Digestives

*This has to be the first in this chapter – the classic chocolate-topped digestive. You can choose whether you prefer milk or dark chocolate.*

**INGREDIENTS** *Makes 12 biscuits*

50g/2oz wholemeal flour
50g/2oz plain flour, plus extra for dusting
100g/4oz fine oatmeal
30g/1oz caster sugar
¼ tsp bicarbonate of soda
100g/4oz butter
2 tbsp milk (optional)
100g/4oz chocolate, broken into pieces

**METHOD**

**1.** Heat the oven to 200°C/400°F/gas 6 and grease or line a large baking sheet.

**2.** Mix together all the dry ingredients. Rub in the butter until the mixture resembles breadcrumbs. Add the milk a drop at a time, stirring vigorously, until the mixture starts to bind together.

**3.** Using your hands, start to bring all the ingredients into a firm dough and knead gently until smooth.

**4.** Roll out the dough to about 5mm/¼in thick and cut into rounds with a 7.5cm/3in biscuit cutter. Place on the prepared baking sheet.

**5.** Bake in the oven for 10–12 minutes until slightly darker around the edges.

**6.** Leave to cool on the baking sheet for 1 minute, then transfer to a wire rack in one layer with a sheet of kitchen paper underneath.

**7.** Melt the chocolate in a heatproof bowl set over a pan of gently simmering water. Remove from the heat.

**8.** Place a teaspoon, flat knife and fork in a mug of boiling water. Using the teaspoon, spoon a little of the chocolate on to each biscuit. Smooth the surface with the knife, then pull the fork through the chocolate to create the traditional pattern. Leave to cool and set.

# Chocolate Chip Cookies

✳ ✳ ✳ ✳ ✳ ✳ ✳ ✳

*There are more cookies in Chapter 6, but this classic seemed to belong here in the chocolate chapter. You can make large or small cookies – smaller ones are more suitable if you have children.*

## INGREDIENTS *Makes 12 cookies*

150g/5oz plain flour, plus extra
   for dusting
½ tsp baking powder
125g/4½oz butter
100g/4oz granulated sugar
40g/2½oz dark brown soft sugar
1 egg
2 tsp vanilla extract
100g/4oz plain chocolate,
   chopped into chunks

## METHOD

**1.** Heat the oven to 200°C/400°F/ gas 6 and grease two large baking sheets.

**2.** Put the flour and baking powder in a bowl and rub in the butter. Stir in the sugars. Add the egg and vanilla and start to mix until the dough begins to pull together. Add the chocolate chunks and continue to knead to a smooth dough.

**3.** Take spoonfuls of the dough, roll into balls, then flatten slightly and place well apart on the prepared baking sheets.

**4.** Bake in the oven for 10–15 minutes until spread and slightly firm around the edges.

**5.** Leave the cookies to cool on the baking sheet for a few minutes until they begin to firm up, then transfer to a wire rack to finish cooling.

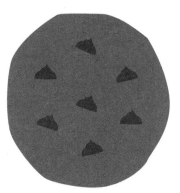

# Chocolate Shortbread

*Sprinkling the shortbread with granulated sugar gives a lovely crunchy finish. Cutting the unbaked dough makes it easier to break when it is cooked.*

**INGREDIENTS** *Makes 24 biscuits*

350g/12oz plain flour
35g/1¼oz cocoa powder
½ tsp ground cinnamon
¼ teaspoon bicarbonate of soda
a pinch of salt
350g/12oz butter
200g/7oz icing sugar, sifted
50g/2oz granulated sugar, for sprinkling

**METHOD**

**1.** Heat the oven to 160°C/325°F/gas 3 and grease and line a shallow 20cm/8in square cake tin.

**2.** Sift together the flour, cocoa, cinnamon, bicarbonate of soda and salt.

**3.** Beat together the butter and icing sugar until pale and creamy. Add to the dry ingredients and mix until just combined. Spread the dough evenly in the prepared cake tin. Chill for about 15 minutes.

**4.** Prick the dough all over with a fork and cut into bars.

**5.** Bake in the oven for 20 minutes until firm.

**6.** While still warm, cut into bars following the marks you made. Sprinkle the top generously with granulated sugar, covering the top completely. Leave to cool completely in the pan, then turn out.

**CHOCOLATE-DIPPED SHORTBREAD**

If you like, you can dip the ends of the biscuits in 75g/3oz chocolate, melted in a heatproof bowl set over a pan of gently simmering water.

# Chocolate & Hazelnut Biscuits

✳ ✳ ✳ ✳ ✳ ✳ ✳ ✳

*You can make these lovely, chunky biscuits with any of your favourite nuts instead of the hazelnuts, if you prefer.*

## INGREDIENTS *Makes 12*

50g/2oz hazelnuts
100g/4oz dark brown soft sugar
75g/3oz plain flour
25g/1oz cocoa powder
60g/2½oz butter
150g/5oz dark chocolate,
    broken into pieces
1 egg, lightly beaten
50g/2oz white chocolate chips

## METHOD

**1.** Heat the oven to 200°C/400°F/ gas 6 and grease and line two baking sheets.
**2.** Toast the hazelnuts in a dry frying pan until just turning golden. Tip out immediately and rub off the skins, if necessary. Leave to cool slightly. Chop roughly, if you like.
**3.** Mix the hazelnuts, sugar, flour and cocoa in a bowl.
**4.** Melt the butter and chocolate in a small pan over a low heat, stirring just until smooth. Remove from the heat and pour into the biscuit mixture. Stir together until blended, adding the egg and finally the chocolate chips. Take spoonfuls of the mixture and place, slightly apart, on the prepared baking sheets.
**5.** Bake in the oven for 10 minutes until just firm.
**6.** Leave to cool on the baking sheets for 1 minute, then transfer to a wire rack to finish cooling.

# Chocolate Roll Biscuits

*These neat little biscuits are made by rolling together a plain and a chocolate dough for a pretty effect. Make sure the dough is not too dry or it will be difficult to roll.*

## INGREDIENTS

*Makes 10 large biscuits*

100g/4oz butter
100g/4oz caster sugar
1 egg, separated
225g/8oz self-raising flour, plus extra for dusting
1 tbsp cocoa powder
2–3 tbsp milk

## METHOD

**1.** Beat together the butter and sugar until pale and creamy. Reserve 1 tbsp of the egg white and beat the remaining egg. Gradually work it into the creamed mixture with the flour and mix to a firm dough, adding a little of the milk, if necessary. Divide the dough in half and mix the cocoa into one half, again adding a little milk, if needed.

**2.** Roll out each piece on a lightly floured surface to a rectangle about 23×13cm/9×5in, pressing the edges to neaten. Brush one piece with the reserved egg white and place the other on top. Roll up tightly from the long side. Wrap in clingfilm and chill for 30 minutes.

**3.** Heat the oven to 190°C/375°F/gas 5 and grease or line a large baking sheet.

**4.** Cut the dough into 2.5cm/1in slices and arrange cut-side up on the prepared baking sheet.

**5.** Bake in the oven for about 20 minutes until firm.

**6.** Leave to cool on the baking sheet for 1 minute, then transfer to a wire rack to finish cooling.

# Double Chocolate Chip Crunch

✳ ✳ ✳ ✳ ✳ ✳ ✳ ✳

*These are testament to the fact that you can never have too much chocolate. Change the chocolate chunks to milk or white chocolate, if you prefer.*

**INGREDIENTS** *Makes 12 biscuits*

250g/9oz plain flour, plus extra
   for dusting
½ tsp bicarbonate of soda
125g/5oz butter
75g/3oz light brown soft sugar
75g/3oz cocoa powder
1 egg, lightly beaten
½ tsp vanilla extract
175g/6oz dark chocolate,
   cut into chunks

**METHOD**

**1.** Put the flour and bicarbonate of soda in a bowl. Rub in the butter until the mixture resembles coarse breadcrumbs. Stir in the sugar and cocoa. Add the egg and vanilla, then mix to a firm dough. Cover with clingfilm and chill for 30 minutes or overnight, if possible.

**2.** Heat the oven to 180°C/350°F/ gas 4 and grease or line two baking sheets.

**3.** Shape the mixture into small balls with lightly floured hands, flatten slightly, and arrange well apart on the prepared baking sheets.

**4.** Bake in the oven for about 10 minutes until firm and darker round the edges.

**5.** Leave to cool on the baking sheet for 1 minute, then transfer to a wire rack to finish cooling.

# White Chocolate & Almond Biscuits

✻ ✻ ✻ ✻ ✻ ✻ ✻ ✻

*Great chunks of white chocolate adorn these mouth-wateringly sweet biscuits, made with lots of delicious ground almonds – a great item in the baker's storecupboard.*

**INGREDIENTS** *Makes 16 biscuits*

150g/5oz plain flour, plus extra
   for dusting
100g/4oz ground almonds
½ tsp bicarbonate of soda
a pinch of salt
100g/4oz butter
150g/5oz caster sugar
1 egg
1 tsp almond extract
100g/4oz white chocolate,
   cut into chunks

**METHOD**

**1.** Heat the oven to 190°C/375°F/ gas 4 and grease or line two baking sheets.

**2.** Put the flour, ground almonds, bicarbonate of soda and salt in a bowl. Rub in the butter until the mixture resembles coarse breadcrumbs. Stir in the sugar. Add the egg and almond extract and start mixing, then tip in the chocolate chunks and mix to a firm dough.

**3.** Shape the mixture into small balls with lightly floured hands, flatten slightly, then place, slightly apart, on the prepared baking sheets.

**4.** Bake in the oven for about 15 minutes until golden brown.

**5.** Leave to cool on the baking sheet for 1 minute, then transfer to a wire rack to finish cooling.

# Mint Chocolate & Ginger Biscuits

✳ ✳ ✳ ✳ ✳ ✳ ✳ ✳

*Ginger and mint make a great flavour combination. This recipe makes chunky little biscuits with a minty chocolate topping.*

**INGREDIENTS** *Makes 12 biscuits*

100g/4oz plain flour, plus extra
  for dusting
2 tsp baking powder
1 tsp ground ginger
50g/2oz butter
50g/2oz honey
1–2 tbsp stem ginger syrup
  from the jar
50g/2oz mint chocolate,
  broken into chunks

**METHOD**

**1.** Heat the oven to 180°C/350°F/ gas 4. Grease a large baking sheet.
**2.** Put the flour, baking powder, ginger and butter in a bowl and rub in the butter until the mixture resembles coarse breadcrumbs. Stir in the honey and enough of the syrup to bind the mixture into a soft dough.
**3.** Shape the dough into small balls with lightly floured hands, then place them on the prepared baking sheet. Press them slightly flatter with a fork.
**4.** Bake in the oven for about 10 minutes until darker round the edges.
**5.** Leave on the tray for about 1 minute to harden slightly, then transfer to a wire rack to cool.
**6.** To make the icing, melt the chocolate in a heatproof bowl over a pan of gently simmering water. Spread the chocolate over the biscuits using a palette knife dipped in hot water. Leave to cool and set.

# Lemon & White Chocolate Biscuits

✤ ✤ ✤ ✤ ✤ ✤ ✤

*A light and lemony dough is perfect to contrast with the richness of the white chocolate. Dark chocolate would work too in this recipe.*

**INGREDIENTS** *Makes 12 biscuits*
175g/6oz butter
175g/6oz light brown soft sugar
1 egg, lightly beaten
grated zest and juice of ½ lemon
175g/6oz plain flour
½ tsp bicarbonate of soda
150g/5oz white chocolate chunks

**METHOD**
**1.** Heat the oven to 190°C/375°F/ gas 5 and grease or line two baking sheets.
**2.** Beat together the butter and sugar until pale and creamy. Gradually work in the egg and lemon juice alternately with spoonfuls of the flour with the bicarbonate of soda added. Add the chocolate chunks and mix to a soft dough. Place spoonfuls of the mixture well apart on the prepared baking sheets.
**3.** Bake in the oven for about 10 minutes until just slightly dark around the edges.
**4.** Leave to cool on the baking sheet for 1 minute, then transfer to a wire rack to finish cooling.

# Chilli Chocolate Snaps

❈ ❈ ❈ ❈ ❈ ❈ ❈ ❈

*These delicious biscuits are spiced with chilli, which really enhances the chocolate flavour. Cook them for just 10 minutes if you prefer a chewier biscuit.*

**INGREDIENTS** *Makes 12 biscuits*

100g/4oz butter
225g/8oz dark brown soft sugar
1 tbsp black treacle
1 egg, lightly beaten
175g/6oz rolled oats
100g/4oz plain flour, plus extra
    for dusting
20g/¾oz cocoa powder
2 tsp mild chilli powder
1 tsp bicarbonate of soda
1 tsp ground cinnamon

**METHOD**

**1.** Heat the oven to 190°C/375°F/ gas 5 and grease or line two baking sheets.
**2.** Beat the butter and sugar together until soft and creamy. Beat in the treacle and the egg, followed by the remaining ingredients, then mix to a soft dough.
**3.** Shape into small balls with lightly floured hands, flatten slightly, and arrange well apart on the prepared baking sheets.
**4.** Bake in the oven for about 15 minutes until firm and crisp round the edges.
**5.** Leave to cool on the baking sheet for 1 minute, then transfer to a wire rack to finish cooling.

**CHILLI AND CHOCOLATE**

If you regard chilli in a sweet biscuit with trepidation, use just 1 tsp of chilli powder at first and see if you like the kick of heat enough to increase it next time.

# Chocolate Orange Sandwich Biscuits

*You can make these small or large, filled or plain – whichever way you prepare them, they are deliciously crumbly.*

**INGREDIENTS** *Makes 12 biscuits*

150g/5oz butter
15g/½oz icing sugar, sifted
100g/4oz plain flour
15g/½oz cornflour
15g/½oz cocoa powder

FOR THE FILLING

60g/2½oz butter
75g/3oz icing sugar, sifted
2 tsp grated orange zest

**METHOD**

**1.** Heat the oven to 180°C/350°F/gas 4 and grease or line two baking sheets.

**2.** Beat the butter and sugar together until pale and creamy, then mix in the flour, cornflour and cocoa.

**3.** Spoon the mixture into a piping bag with a small nozzle and pipe 24 little whirls on to the prepared baking sheets.

**4.** Bake in the oven for about 12 minutes until just firm and slightly darker round the edges.

**5.** Leave to cool on the baking sheet for 1 minute, then transfer to a wire rack to finish cooling.

**6.** For the filling, beat the butter, icing sugar and orange zest until smooth and creamy and use to sandwich the biscuits together in pairs.

# Chocolate Crinkles

✳ ✳ ✳ ✳ ✳ ✳ ✳ ✳

*Soft and chewy little domed biscuits, these have a dusting of icing sugar to display the beautiful cracked surface to perfection.*

## INGREDIENTS *Makes 20 biscuits*

75g/3oz dark chocolate,
   cut into chunks
40g/1½oz butter
50g/2oz dark brown soft sugar
1 egg
½ tsp vanilla extract
1 tsp strong coffee powder
75g/3oz plain flour
¼ tsp baking powder
15g/½oz icing sugar, sifted, plus
   extra for sprinkling

## METHOD

**1.** Melt the chocolate, butter and sugar in a heatproof bowl set over a pan of gently simmering water.
**2.** In a separate bowl, beat together the egg, vanilla and coffee. Add the chocolate mixture, then stir in the flour and baking powder and mix to a soft dough. Chill in the fridge for at least 1 hour.

**3.** Heat the oven to 160°C/325°F/ gas 3 and grease or line a large baking sheet.
**4.** With lightly floured hands, shape the dough into 20 small balls. Put the sifted icing sugar in a shallow soup plate. Add a few balls at a time and roll them round the bowl to coat in the sugar, then arrange them well apart on the prepared baking sheet.
**5.** Bake in the oven for 12 minutes until cracked on top and darkening round the edges.
**6.** Leave to cool on the baking sheet for 1 minute, then transfer to a wire rack to finish cooling. Sprinkle with icing sugar.

# Chocolate Espresso Cookies

✳ ✳ ✳ ✳ ✳ ✳ ✳ ✳

*Dark and rich-tasting, these are definitely at the sophisticated end of the biscuit spectrum – one to accompany your espresso.*

**INGREDIENTS** *Makes 24 cookies*

50g/2oz plain flour, plus extra
  for dusting
¼ tsp baking powder
a pinch of salt
300g/11oz dark chocolate,
  cut into chunks
4 tbsp coconut oil
2 eggs
250g/9oz caster sugar
1½ tsp instant espresso granules
1 tsp vanilla extract
sea salt flakes

**METHOD**

**1.** Mix the flour, baking powder and salt in a bowl.
**2.** Melt the chocolate with the oil in a heatproof bowl set over a pan of gently simmering water. Remove from the heat and leave to cool slightly.

**3.** Beat together the eggs, sugar, espresso granules and vanilla until pale and creamy and the batter trails off the whisk in thick ribbons. Stir the melted chocolate mixture into the flour, then fold in the beaten eggs and mix to a soft dough. Chill for 30 minutes.
**4.** Heat the oven to 180°C/350°F/ gas 4 and grease and line two baking sheets.
**5.** With lightly floured hands, shape the mixture into walnut-sized balls and place well apart on the prepared baking sheets.
**6.** Bake in the oven for 10 minutes until firm round the edges but still soft in the centre.
**7.** Leave to cool on the baking sheets for 1 minute, then transfer to a wire rack to finish cooling.

# Chunky Chocolate Bars

�֍ �֍ ✷ ✷ ✷ ✷ ✷ ✷

*For these powerful, nutty, chocolatey and crunchy bars you can use any kind of chocolate or biscuits and put together your own unique treats.*

## INGREDIENTS *Makes 10 bars* ❄️

100g/4oz butter

250g/9oz dark chocolate, broken into chunks

3 tbsp golden syrup

100g/4oz ginger biscuits, broken into chunks

50g/2oz digestive biscuits, broken into chunks

100g/4oz milk chocolate chips

100g/4oz white chocolate chips

50g/2oz mini marshmallows

## METHOD

**1.** Melt the butter, chocolate and syrup in a pan over a low heat, stirring.

**2.** Remove from the heat and add the biscuits, stirring until they are well coated. Leave to cool a little while you line a 20cm/8in square tin with baking paper.

**3.** Stir the chocolate chips and marshmallows into the chocolate mixture, then press into the prepared tin, leave to cool, and chill in the fridge for about 3 hours until firm.

**4.** Cut into bars to serve.

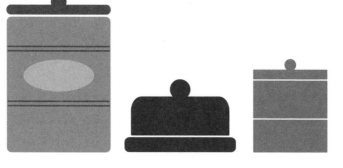

# Bourbon Biscuits

*I couldn't decide whether these old favourites should go into the chocolate, classic or fancy chapter! No one I baked them for was very bothered – they were too intent on enjoying the biscuits.*

**INGREDIENTS** *Makes 12 biscuits*

200g/7oz plain flour, plus extra for dusting
25g/1oz cocoa powder
a pinch of salt
75g/3oz butter
75g/3oz caster sugar
1 egg, lightly beaten
a few drops of vanilla extract
1 tbsp milk

FOR THE FILLING

50g/2oz plain chocolate, broken into chunks
25g/1oz butter
50g/2oz icing sugar, sifted

**METHOD**

**1.** Heat the oven to 190°C/325°F/gas 5 and grease or line a large baking sheet.

**2.** Put the flour, cocoa and salt into a bowl and rub in the butter until the mixture resembles coarse breadcrumbs. Stir in the sugar. Mix in the egg and vanilla to form a fairly stiff dough.

**3.** Roll out on a lightly floured surface to about 5mm/¼in thick and cut into 24 rectangles, or circles using a 5cm/2in biscuit cutter. Place on the prepared baking sheet.

**4.** Bake in the oven for about 12 minutes until firm.

**5.** Leave to cool on the baking sheet for 1 minute, then transfer to a wire rack to finish cooling.

**6.** Meanwhile, melt the chocolate and butter in a heatproof bowl set over a pan of gently simmering water. Remove from the heat and stir in the icing sugar, then beat well until smooth and thick.

**7.** Sandwich the biscuits together in pairs and leave to cool and set.

# Chocolate & Coconut Clusters

✳ ✳ ✳ ✳ ✳ ✳ ✳ ✳

*Rugged biscuits with a chewy centre, these are great for the lunch box. Replace the cocoa with a little more flour if you prefer.*

**INGREDIENTS** *Makes 12 clusters*

50g/2oz butter
100g/4oz clear honey
100g/4oz rolled oats
75g/3oz desiccated coconut
15g/½oz cocoa powder
1 egg, beaten
1 tbsp plain flour

**METHOD**

**1.** Heat the oven to 180°C/350°F/ gas 4 and grease or line a large baking sheet.

**2.** Melt the butter and honey in a pan over a low heat. Remove from the heat and stir in the oats, coconut and cocoa. Gradually add enough beaten egg to make a soft dough.

**3.** Place spoonfuls of the mixture well apart on the prepared baking sheet.

**4.** Bake in the oven for about 15 minutes until shiny and moist-looking.

**5.** Leave to cool on the baking sheet for 1 minute, then transfer to a wire rack to finish cooling.

# CHAPTER 4

✳✳✳✳✳✳✳✳✳

# FRUIT & NUT BISCUITS

Some of my favourites are included here, such as Anzac biscuits and garibaldi. The latter are much easier to make than you might expect and, as with all home-made biscuits, you can make them exactly the size you want.

# Luscious & crunchy biscuits

********

Texture is what this chapter is all about – the contrast of the crunchy nuts, the smooth dough and the oases of light and luscious fruit.

Common biscuit ingredients such as ground almonds, sultanas, raisins and apricots are brilliantly adaptable items to keep in your cupboard and use in your biscuit-making. But don't limit yourself to always using the same ingredients – branch out and experiment with some of the more unusual options, such as mango, pistachios, prunes or pineapple.

Remember to store dried fruit and nuts carefully. Although they are intended to be kept for some time in the storecupboard, make sure that you put them in an airtight bag or sealed plastic container otherwise fruit will become hard and nuts will go stale, when they will taste musty and unpleasant.

**REDUCING THE SUGAR**

As sugar has little nutritional value, you may want to cut down on the sugar content in your diet. The first way to do this is to avoid processed foods, which contain sugar in the most unlikely places, both savoury and sweet, and make your own from scratch instead. You can also substitute other ingredients for processed sugar in cakes and biscuits, such as honey, agave syrup, puréed prunes, unsweetened, stewed dessert apples or maple syrup.

# Anzac Biscuits

✳ ✳ ✳ ✳ ✳ ✳ ✳ ✳

*Brought to us from New Zealand and Australia, these combine oats with coconut for a delicious, crunchy biscuit with a lovely syrupy sweetness.*

**INGREDIENTS** *Makes 12 biscuits*

60g/2½oz plain flour, plus extra
   for sprinkling
50g/2oz rolled oats
25g/1oz desiccated coconut
75g/3oz butter
50g/2oz caster sugar
1 tbsp golden syrup
½ tsp bicarbonate of soda
2 tsp hot water

**METHOD**

**1.** Heat the oven to 160°C/325°F/
gas 3 and grease or line two
baking sheets.
**2.** Mix the flour, oats and coconut
in a bowl.
**3.** Melt the butter, sugar and syrup
in a small pan over a low heat.
Pour into the dry ingredients. Mix
the bicarbonate of soda with the
hot water and add it to the bowl,
stirring to mix everything together

thoroughly and to cool the dough.
**4.** With lightly floured hands, shape
the mixture into about 12 balls and
arrange them well apart on the
prepared baking sheets. You can
make smaller biscuits if you prefer.
**5.** Bake in the oven for 20 minutes
until golden brown.
**6.** Leave to cool on the baking sheet
for 1 minute, then transfer to a wire
rack to finish cooling.

#  Currant & Lemon Biscuits

## ❊ ❊ ❊ ❊ ❊ ❊ ❊ ❊

*Made from a very thin batter, these are rather like drop scones. Some of the butter leaks out during baking but this gives a crisp edge.*

**INGREDIENTS** *Makes 8 biscuits*
40g/1½oz butter
1 tbsp maple syrup
1 egg, lightly beaten
grated zest and juice of ½ lemon
50g/2oz wholemeal flour
3 tbsp currants

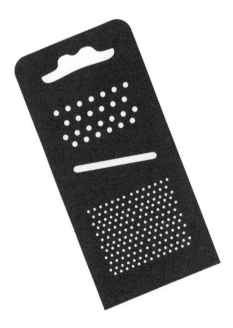

**METHOD**
**1.** Heat the oven to 200°C/400°F/ gas 6 and grease and line a large baking sheet.
**2.** Beat the butter until pale and creamy, then beat in the maple syrup. Gradually work in the egg, then the lemon zest and juice, the flour and the currants. Mix to a loose batter. Drop spoonfuls of the batter well apart on the prepared baking sheet.
**3.** Bake in the oven for 10 minutes until golden brown and dark at the edges.
**4.** Leave to cool on the baking sheet for 1 minute, then transfer to a wire rack to finish cooling.

# Garibaldi

✾ ✾ ✾ ✾ ✾ ✾ ✾ ✾

*A biscuit collection would not be complete without 'squashed fly biscuits', first made in 1861 and named after the military leader and politician who was the central figure in the reunification of Italy – a historic biscuit, in fact!*

**INGREDIENTS** *Makes 12 biscuits*

175g/6oz plain flour, plus extra
  for dusting
a pinch of salt
40g/1½oz butter
40g/1½oz caster sugar
3 tbsp milk
1 egg, lightly beaten
50g/2oz currants
2 tsp demerara sugar (optional)

**METHOD**

**1.** Heat the oven to 190°C/375°F/ gas 5 and grease a large baking sheet.
**2.** Put the flour and salt in a bowl and rub in the butter until the mixture resembles coarse breadcrumbs. Stir in the sugar, then add enough milk to mix to a soft dough.

**3.** Roll out on a lightly floured surface to about 30×30cm (12×12in). Brush with the beaten egg. Sprinkle half the dough with the currants and demerara sugar, if using, then fold the other half of the dough over the top.
**4.** Roll out very gently to flatten the dough slightly. Cut into 12 biscuits, using a square biscuit cutter or a pizza wheel if you have one, trimming the edges if you like. Transfer carefully to the prepared baking sheet and brush with beaten egg.
**5.** Bake in the oven for about 12 minutes until the glaze is golden.
**6.** Leave on the baking sheet for 1 minute to harden, then transfer to a wire rack to finish cooling.

# Date Biscuits

❋ ❋ ❋ ❋ ❋ ❋ ❋ ❋

*These are not the most prepossessing of biscuits, being a mottled brown colour, but they taste delicious and are one of my favourites.*

**INGREDIENTS** *Makes 12 biscuits*
150g/5oz plain flour, plus extra for dusting
½ tsp bicarbonate of soda
75g/3oz dark brown soft sugar
50g/2oz stoned dates, chopped
½ tsp mixed spice
75g/3oz butter

**METHOD**
**1.** Heat the oven to 180°C/350°F/ gas 4 and grease two baking sheets.
**2.** Put all the ingredients in a large bowl and beat to a smooth dough, or just blitz them in a food processor.
**3.** Roll out on a lightly floured surface to about 5mm/¼in thick and cut into rounds with a medium-sized biscuit cutter. Arrange on the prepared baking sheet.
**4.** Bake in the oven for 10 minutes until firm, slightly brown, and darker around the edges.
**5.** Leave to cool on the baking sheet for 1 minute, then transfer to a wire rack to finish cooling.

# Walnut Crunch

❄ ❄ ❄ ❄ ❄ ❄ ❄

*These are made by the melting method and produce delicious little rounded biscuits, crunchy with walnuts – although you could use other nuts, if preferred.*

**INGREDIENTS** *Makes 12 biscuits*
50g/2oz plain chocolate
50g/2oz butter
100g/4oz caster sugar
1 egg
1 tsp vanilla extract
50g/2oz plain flour
¼ tsp baking powder
175g/6oz walnut halves, coarsely
   chopped
icing sugar, sifted, for sprinkling

**METHOD**
**1.** Heat the oven to 180°C/350°F/ gas 4 and grease or line two baking sheets.
**2.** Melt the chocolate in a heatproof bowl set over a pan of gently simmering water.
**3.** Beat the butter, sugar and chocolate together until light and creamy. Gradually beat in the egg and vanilla, then fold in the flour, baking powder and walnuts and mix to a soft dough.
**4.** Place spoonfuls of the mixture well apart on the baking sheets.
**5.** Bake in the oven for 10 minutes until firm and darker round the edges.
**6.** Leave to cool on the baking sheet for 1 minute, then transfer to a wire rack to finish cooling. Serve dusted with icing sugar.

# Soft Fig Biscuits

✿ ✿ ✿ ✿ ✿ ✿ ✿ ✿

*These can be quickly put together by whizzing everything in the food processor, rolling out and baking. Deliciously crumbly, they are irresistible.*

**INGREDIENTS** *Makes 12 biscuits*

100g/4oz plain flour, plus extra
  for dusting
50g/2oz rolled oats
½ tsp bicarbonate of soda
100g/4oz dark brown soft sugar
100g/4oz figs, stems trimmed and
  flesh chopped
1 tsp ground ginger
100g/4oz butter
1 tbsp icing sugar

**METHOD**

**1.** Heat the oven to 180°C/350°F/
gas 4 and grease two baking sheets.
**2.** Put all the ingredients in a bowl
and beat to a smooth dough, or blitz
them in a food processor.
**3.** Roll out on a lightly floured
surface to about 5mm/¼in thick.
Cut into rounds with a medium-sized
biscuit cutter, then arrange them

on the prepared baking sheets.
**4.** Bake in the oven for 10 minutes
until firm, slightly brown, and darker
around the edges.
**5.** Leave to cool on the baking sheet
for 1 minute, then transfer to a wire
rack to finish cooling. Sift the icing
sugar over while still warm.

# Light Lemon Biscuits

✻ ✻ ✻ ✻ ✻ ✻ ✻ ✻

*The sharp flavour of lemon contrasts with the sweet, buttery biscuits, giving a mouth-watering result that could not be easier to achieve.*

**INGREDIENTS** *Makes 12 biscuits*
150g/5oz butter
100g/4oz caster sugar
1 tbsp finely grated lemon zest
225g/8oz plain flour
1 tbsp demerara sugar

**METHOD**
**1.** Beat the butter, caster sugar and lemon zest together until pale and creamy. Gradually work in the flour and mix to a firm dough. Shape into a long roll about 7.5cm/3in in diameter and roll in the demerara sugar. Wrap in clingfilm, then chill for 30 minutes.
**2.** Heat the oven to 160°C/325°F/ gas 3 and grease or line a large baking sheet.
**3.** Cut the roll into about 12 biscuits and arrange slightly apart on the prepared baking sheet. Prick lightly with a fork.
**4.** Bake in the oven for 20 minutes until golden brown around the edges.
**5.** Leave to cool on the baking sheet for 1 minute, then transfer to a wire rack to finish cooling.

# Fig & Almond Shortbread

✳ ✳ ✳ ✳ ✳ ✳ ✳ ✳

*This makes a lovely rich and buttery shortbread which cuts into wedges if you make it in a round tin, or bars if you use a square one.*

## INGREDIENTS *Makes 8 bars*

100g/4oz butter
50g/2oz dark brown soft sugar
100g/4oz ground almonds
100g/4oz plain flour
1 tbsp maple syrup
100g/4oz figs, stalks trimmed,
    then chopped

## METHOD

**1.** Heat the oven to 180°C/350°F/gas 4 and grease and line a shallow 18cm/7in cake tin.

**2.** Beat the butter until soft, then beat in the sugar, ground almonds, flour and maple syrup.

**3.** Press half the mixture into the prepared cake tin, then sprinkle in the figs. Cover with the remaining dough and smooth it over the figs, using the back of a spoon dipped in flour. Prick the surface with a fork and cut into wedges or bars with a sharp knife.

**4.** Bake in the oven for about 20 minutes until golden brown.

**5.** Leave to cool in the tin for 5 minutes, then transfer to a wire rack to finish cooling.

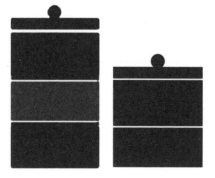

# Mango Biscuits

*I love the flavour of mango, so I decided to experiment with some dried mango in a biscuit. These are quite solid biscuits with a subtle mango flavour. Chop the mangoes quite finely for the best results.*

**INGREDIENTS** *Makes 12 biscuits*

100g/4oz plain flour, plus extra for dusting
75g/3oz clear honey
2 tbsp golden syrup
50g/2oz dried mango, finely chopped
1 tsp ground cinnamon
1 tbsp sunflower oil

**METHOD**

**1.** Heat the oven to 200°C/400°F/gas 6 and grease or line a large baking sheet.

**2.** Put all the ingredients in a large bowl and beat to a smooth dough.

**3.** Roll out on a lightly floured surface to about 5mm/¼in thick and cut out with a square biscuit cutter. Arrange on the prepared baking sheet.

**4.** Bake in the oven for 12 minutes until golden brown.

**5.** Leave to cool on the baking sheet for 1 minute, then transfer to a wire rack to finish cooling.

**SQUARE CUTTERS**

It can be hard to find square rather than round cutters in the shops – even cookware stores often don't have them – but they are easy to find online from major suppliers or in children's bakeware sets.

# Banana Biscuits

✳ ✳ ✳ ✳ ✳ ✳ ✳ ✳

*Such an easy recipe for a chunky biscuit with a soft centre,
this is one to use up a banana that is very ripe –
something that never need be wasted.*

**INGREDIENTS** *Makes 12 biscuits*

100g/4oz plain flour
25g/1oz wholemeal flour
75g/3oz butter
2 tbsp golden syrup
1 banana, mashed
1 tsp vanilla extract
1 tsp mixed spice
1 egg, lightly beaten
50g/2oz plain flour
50g/2oz chopped mixed nuts

**INSTANT LUNCH**
You can pop a frozen biscuit in
a lunch box in the morning and
it will be defrosted and ready
to eat by lunch time.

**METHOD**

**1.** Heat the oven to 180°C/350°F/
gas 4 and grease or line a large
baking sheet.

**2.** Put the flours in a bowl and
rub in the butter until the mixture
resembles coarse breadcrumbs. Stir
in the syrup, banana, vanilla, spice,
egg, flour and nuts and mix to a
soft dough.

**3.** Place spoonfuls of the mixture
slightly apart on the prepared
baking sheet.

**4.** Bake in the oven for about
15 minutes until golden brown.

**5.** Leave to cool on the baking sheet
for 1 minute, then transfer to a wire
rack to finish cooling.

# Macadamia Nut Biscuits

## ❄ ❄ ❄ ❄ ❄ ❄ ❄

*These deliciously chunky biscuits can be made with whole nuts or chopped nuts, as you prefer. As with most nutty biscuits, you can also try the recipe with different types of nut.*

**INGREDIENTS** *Makes 12 biscuits*

225g/8oz butter
200g/7oz caster sugar
200g/7oz light brown soft sugar
1 egg
1 tsp vanilla extract
225g/8oz plain flour, plus extra
   for dusting
1 tsp bicarbonate of soda
100g/4oz macadamia nuts,
   whole or halved
90ml/3fl oz warm water

**METHOD**

**1.** Heat the oven to 180°C/350°F/
gas 4 and grease or line two
baking sheets.
**2.** Beat the butter and sugars
together until pale and creamy.
Gradually work in the egg, vanilla,
flour, bicarbonate of soda and
nuts, and add enough of the warm
water to mix to a soft dough.
**3.** Shape into small balls with lightly
floured hands, flatten slightly, and
arrange well apart on the prepared
baking sheets.
**4.** Bake in the oven for about
8 minutes until golden brown
around the edges.
**5.** Leave to cool on the baking sheet
for 1 minute, then transfer to a wire
rack to finish cooling.

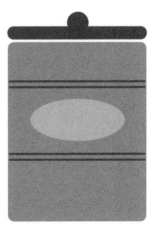

# Peanut Butter Windows

✽ ✽ ✽ ✽ ✽ ✽ ✽ ✽

*This is one for all lovers of peanut butter – either smooth or crunchy will work just as well. The redcurrant jelly gives a nice contrast in flavour and texture.*

**INGREDIENTS** *Makes 8 biscuits*
250g/9oz plain flour, plus extra
   for sprinkling
a pinch of salt
200g/7oz butter
75g/3oz caster sugar
1 egg, lightly beaten
1 tsp vanilla extract
grated zest of ½ lemon
a pinch of salt
FOR THE FILLING
2 tbsp redcurrant jelly
3 tbsp peanut butter

**METHOD**
**1.** Heat the oven to 160°C/325°F/
gas 3 and grease or line a large
baking sheet.
**2.** Put the flour and salt in a bowl.
Rub in the butter until the mixture
resembles coarse breadcrumbs,
then stir in the sugar. Add the egg,
vanilla, lemon zest and salt and mix
to a firm dough.
**3.** Roll out on a lightly floured
surface to about 5mm/¼in thick and
cut into 16 squares with a 5cm/2in
biscuit cutter. Use a petit four cutter
or small shape cutter to take a
diamond out of the centre of half
of the biscuits. Reroll the trimmings
as necessary.
**4.** Arrange the whole biscuits on the
prepared baking sheet. Spread the
redcurrant jelly thinly over each
biscuit and top with a spoonful of
peanut butter, then lay the biscuits
with the hole in them on top.
**5.** Bake in the oven for 15 minutes
until golden brown.
**6.** Leave to cool on the baking sheet
for 1 minute, then transfer to a wire
rack to finish cooling.

# Almond Shortbread

*To translate these into gluten-free biscuits, substitute gluten-free flour for the plain flour, or make them entirely from ground almonds.*

**INGREDIENTS** *Makes 8 bars*

100g/4oz butter
50g/2oz caster sugar
100g/4oz ground almonds
100g/4oz plain flour
caster sugar for sprinkling (optional)

**METHOD**

**1.** Heat the oven to 180°C/350°F/gas 4 and grease and line a 20cm/8in square cake tin.

**2.** Beat the butter until soft, then beat in the sugar, ground almonds and flour.

**3.** Press the mixture into the prepared cake tin, prick with a fork and cut into bars with a sharp knife.

**4.** Bake in the oven for about 20 minutes until golden brown.

**5.** Leave to cool in the tin for 5 minutes, then transfer to a wire rack to finish cooling. If you like, you can sprinkle the shortbread with caster sugar either before or after baking. Finally, cut the bars again.

# Nut & Honey Biscuits

*Use a good-quality honey to give a strong and distinctive flavour to this traditional sandwich biscuit with a nutty topping.*

**INGREDIENTS** *Makes 12 biscuits*

175g/6oz butter
2 tbsp clear honey
¼ tsp almond extract
200g/7oz plain flour, plus extra for dusting
25g/1oz icing sugar, sifted
50g/2oz almonds, chopped

FOR THE FILLING

50g/2oz butter
1 tbsp clear honey
100g/4oz icing sugar, sifted

**METHOD**

**1.** Heat the oven to 160°C/325°F/gas 3 and grease or line two baking sheets.

**2.** Beat the butter and honey together until pale and creamy. Gradually work in the almond extract, flour and icing sugar and mix to a soft dough. Cover and chill for 30 minutes.

**3.** Shape into 24 small balls with lightly floured hands, flatten slightly, and arrange well apart on the prepared baking sheets. Sprinkle half the biscuits with the chopped almonds.

**4.** Bake in the oven for 18 minutes until golden brown.

**5.** Leave to cool on the baking sheet for 1 minute, then transfer to a wire rack to finish cooling.

**6.** Beat all the filling ingredients together to make a soft buttercream. Spread over the plain biscuits, then gently press a nutty biscuit on top.

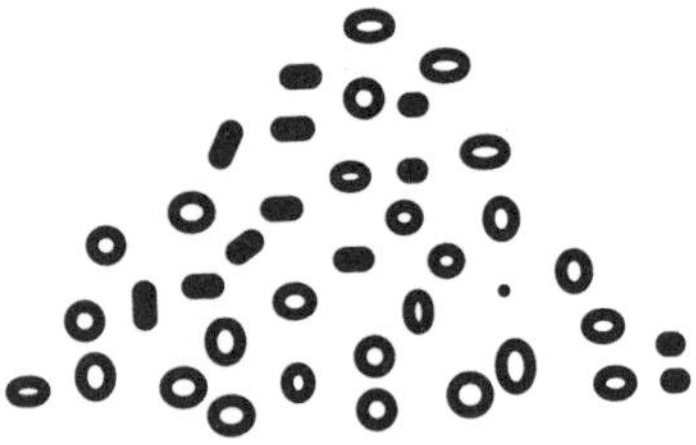

# Hazelnut Snaps

*If you don't have hazelnuts in the cupboard, try these with almonds instead. The icing makes a smooth contrast to the crunchy nuts.*

**INGREDIENTS** *Makes 12 biscuits*

50g/2oz butter
25g/1oz light brown soft sugar
50g/2oz plain flour, plus extra for dusting
50g/2oz ground hazelnuts
1 tbsp milk (optional)
2 tbsp chopped hazelnuts

FOR THE ICING

100g/4oz icing sugar, sifted
1 tbsp ground hazelnuts
50g/2oz butter

**NO BISCUIT CUTTERS?**

If you don't have biscuits cutters, simply cut out a circle freehand, or cut round the top or bottom of a cup.

**METHOD**

**1.** Heat the oven to 160°C/325°C/gas 3 and grease two baking sheets.

**2.** Beat the butter and sugar together until pale and creamy. Gradually work in the flour and ground hazelnuts until you have a fairly firm dough, adding the milk, if necessary, if the dough is too stiff.

**3.** Roll out on a lightly floured surface to about 5mm/¼in thick and cut into rounds with a 7.5cm/3in biscuit cutter. Place on the prepared baking sheets.

**4.** Bake in the oven for 20 minutes until golden.

**5.** Leave to cool for 1 minute, then transfer to a wire rack.

**6.** Beat the icing sugar and ground hazelnuts into the butter until smooth. Spread over the biscuits and decorate with the chopped hazelnuts.

# Pistachio Nut Biscuits

✼ ✼ ✼ ✼ ✼ ✼ ✼ ✼

*I always like the flash of green when you bake with pistachios, in this case in a rugged biscuit, crunchy on the outside and soft on the inside.*

**INGREDIENTS** *Makes 12 biscuits*

100g/4oz stoned prunes
100ml/4fl oz orange juice
100g/4oz wholemeal flour, plus extra
    for dusting
½ tsp bicarbonate of soda
100g/4oz pistachio nuts, chopped
3 tbsp sunflower oil
1 tbsp demerara sugar

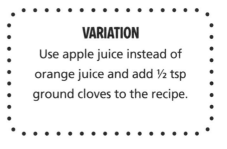

**VARIATION**
Use apple juice instead of
orange juice and add ½ tsp
ground cloves to the recipe.

**METHOD**

**1.** Soak the prunes in the orange juice overnight. Strain, reserving the juice.

**2.** Heat the oven to 180°C/350°F/ gas 4 and grease or line two baking sheets.

**3.** Put all the ingredients except the demerara sugar in a bowl and beat to a smooth dough, adding a little of the soaking juice if necessary.

**4.** Shape into small balls with lightly floured hands, flatten slightly, and arrange well apart on the prepared baking sheets.

**5.** Bake in the oven for about 18 minutes until firm and darker around the edges.

**6.** Leave to cool on the baking sheet for 1 minute, then transfer to a wire rack to finish cooling. Sprinkle with the demerara sugar while still hot.

# Almond Tuiles

✳ ✳ ✳ ✳ ✳ ✳ ✳ ✳

*These are delicate little biscuits which are ideal for serving in style with tea in a pretty cup and saucer or as an accompaniment to a dessert.*

## INGREDIENTS *Makes 18 biscuits*

75g/3oz butter
75g/3oz caster sugar
75g/3oz flaked almonds
50g/2oz plain flour

## METHOD

**1.** Heat the oven to 200°C/400°F/ gas 6 and grease or line a large baking sheet.

**2.** Beat the butter and sugar together until pale and creamy. Stir in the flaked almonds, then gradually work in the flour. Drop spoonfuls of the mixture on the prepared baking sheet.

**3.** Bake in the oven for about 8 minutes until golden and darker round the edges.

**4.** Leave to cool on the baking sheet for 1 minute, then transfer to a wire rack to finish cooling.

# Crumbly Rice Biscuits

❋ ❋ ❋ ❋ ❋ ❋ ❋ ❋

*Just slightly sweet and with a subtle touch of vanilla, these are quite chunky biscuits that go equally with sweet flavours or with cheese.*

## INGREDIENTS *Makes 12 biscuits*

50g/2oz plain flour, plus extra
   for dusting
50g/2oz wholemeal flour
50g/2oz ground almonds
50g/2oz ground rice
½ tsp mixed spice
100g/4oz butter
3 tbsp honey

## METHOD

**1.** Heat the oven to 180°C/350°F/ gas 4 and grease or line a large baking sheet.

**2.** Put the flours, almonds, rice and mixed spice in a bowl and mix together. Rub in the butter until the mixture resembles coarse breadcrumbs. Work in the honey and mix to a slightly crumbly dough.

**3.** Shape into small balls with lightly floured hands, flatten slightly, and arrange well apart on the prepared baking sheet.

**4.** Bake in the oven for about 12 minutes until golden brown.

**5.** Leave to cool on the baking sheet for 1 minute, then transfer to a wire rack to finish cooling.

# CHAPTER 5

\* \* \* \* \* \* \* \* \*

# FANCY BISCUITS

It's fun to make some really interesting biscuits – particularly if you
have special guests – and this is the theme of this section.
You won't find that they are difficult to make, although you
don't need to tell that to your friends!

# Too posh to dunk

❋ ❋ ❋ ❋ ❋ ❋ ❋

These are biscuits to display on your finest china plates rather than with a hearty mug of tea – the sort you used to buy, and will now be able to make, for special treats (although there are a couple especially for dunking).

When you come to this section, get out the doilies and that cake stand that you so rarely use, because it contains some impressive offerings. Having said that, this is a book of traditional recipes and they tend to be practical and easy to make, so there are no complicated and time-consuming options.

Not only will your friends be pleased by the fact that you have made biscuits specially for them, homemade biscuits are usually larger, and often richer, than shop-bought ones, so your spread of goodies will strike them as particularly handsome.

To make it easier to put together delicious recipes at a moment's notice, you might want to keep a few things in your store cupboard, fridge or freezer.

- ❋ **Basics:** flour, bicarbonate of soda.
- ❋ **Fridge staples:** eggs, butter.
- ❋ **Freezer:** puff pastry, filo pastry.
- ❋ **Dried fruits:** sultanas, glacé cherries, mango, dates, figs.
- ❋ **Nuts:** hazelnuts, almonds, ground almonds.
- ❋ **Spices:** cinnamon, mixed spice, ginger.
- ❋ **Sweet things:** sugar, honey, syrup.

With a well-stocked store cupboard, all your cooking will become much easier.

# Florentines

✳ ✳ ✳ ✳ ✳ ✳ ✳ ✳

*Full of crunchy ingredients, fruity and sweet, these delicious biscuits are a special-occasion classic that everyone enjoys.*

**INGREDIENTS** *Makes 12 biscuits*
100g/4oz butter
175g/6oz dark brown soft sugar
250ml/8fl oz double cream
225g/8oz hazelnuts, chopped
300g/11oz flaked almonds
150g/5oz sultanas
1 tbsp plain flour

**METHOD**
**1.** Heat the oven to 180°C/350°F/ gas 4 and grease or line two baking sheets.
**2.** Bring the butter, sugar and cream to the boil in a pan, then remove from the heat and stir in the remaining ingredients.
**3.** Place spoonfuls of the mixture well apart on the prepared baking sheets.
**4.** Bake in the oven for about 10 minutes until golden brown around the edges.
**5.** Leave to cool on the baking sheet for 1 minute, then transfer to a wire rack to finish cooling.

**CHOCOLATE ON TOP**

If you like Chocolate Florentines, simply melt 75g/3oz chocolate in a heatproof bowl set over a pan of gently simmering water then spoon it over the top of the biscuits. Spread evenly and mark into a pattern with a fork dipped in hot water.

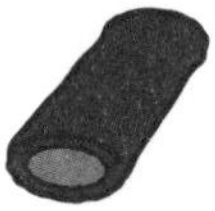

# Brandy Snaps

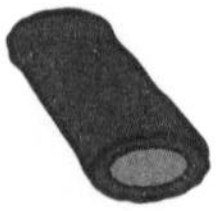

*Very versatile biscuits that make a special tea-time treat, brandy snaps are also suitable for a dessert with ice cream or mousse, especially if they are filled with whipped cream.*

**INGREDIENTS** *Makes 12 snaps*

75g/3oz butter
75g/3oz caster sugar
3 tbsp golden syrup
80g/3¼oz plain flour
1 tsp ground ginger
2 tsp brandy
150ml/5fl oz double cream

**METHOD**

**1.** Heat the oven to 180°C/350°F/ gas 4 and grease or line a large baking sheet.

**2.** Melt the butter, sugar and syrup in a pan, then mix in the remaining ingredients except the cream. Place spoonfuls well apart on the prepared baking sheet.

**3.** Bake in the oven for about 8 minutes until golden brown.

**4.** Grease the handle of a wooden spoon. Loosen the snaps from the baking sheet. Take one at a time and roll it round the spoon handle, then place on a wire rack to cool and harden. If the biscuits become too cool and therefore hard to mould, pop them back in the oven to soften. Leave to cool.

**5.** Whisk the cream until stiff, then spoon into a piping bag. Pipe the cream into the centre of the brandy snap rolls.

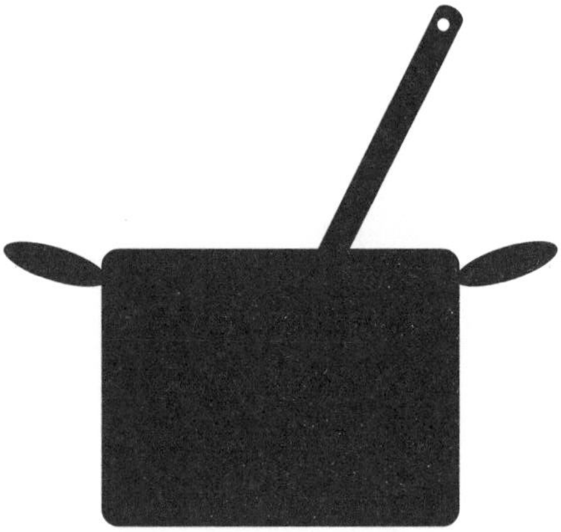

# Cranberry Dodgers

*Jammie Dodgers are popular with both children and adults. Here they've been given a twist as I've used a cranberry sauce to give a slightly sharper flavour.*

**INGREDIENTS** *Makes 8 biscuits*

250g/9oz plain flour, plus extra for sprinkling
a pinch of salt
200g/7oz butter
75g/3oz caster sugar
1 egg, lightly beaten
1 tsp vanilla extract
grated zest of ½ lemon
3 tbsp cranberry sauce or jelly

**METHOD**

**1.** Heat the oven to 160°C/325°F/gas 3 and grease or line two baking sheets.

**2.** Put the flour and salt in a bowl. Rub in the butter until the mixture resembles coarse breadcrumbs, then stir in the sugar. Add the egg, vanilla and lemon zest and mix to a firm dough.

**3.** Roll out on a lightly floured surface to about 5mm/¼in thick and cut into 16 rounds with a 7.5cm/3in biscuit cutter. Use a petit four cutter or small shape cutter to take a circle out of the centre of half the biscuits. Reroll the dough as necessary.

**4.** Arrange the whole biscuits on the prepared baking sheets. Place a spoonful of cranberry sauce on each one, keeping it away from the edges, then put the biscuits with the hole in on top.

**5.** Bake in the oven for 12 minutes until golden brown round the edges.

**6.** Leave to cool on the baking sheet for 1 minute, then transfer to a wire rack to finish cooling.

# Viennese Whirls

*These light and airy biscuits are shaped by piping the mixture on to the baking sheet. You can sandwich them together in pairs with Vanilla Cream (see page 132) if you wish.*

**INGREDIENTS** *Makes 12 biscuits*
150g/5oz butter
100g/4oz plain flour
50g/2oz cornflour
½ tsp vanilla extract

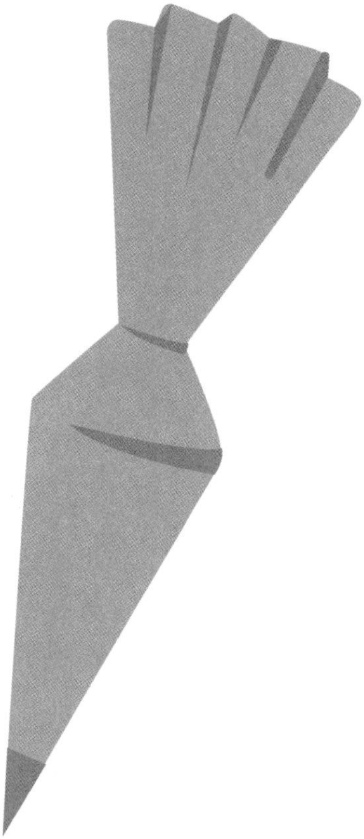

**METHOD**

**1.** Heat the oven to 190°C/375°F/ gas 5 and grease or line a large baking sheet.

**2.** Put all the ingredients in a large bowl and beat to a smooth dough.

**3.** Spoon into a piping bag with a large nozzle and pipe spirals on the prepared baking sheet.

**4.** Bake in the oven for about 12 minutes until golden brown.

**5.** Leave to cool on the baking sheet for 1 minute, then transfer to a wire rack to finish cooling.

# Iced Ginger Shortbread

*Here's an interesting combination of stem ginger chunks with glacé icing on a rich, buttery biscuit. Chop or grate the stem ginger quite finely.*

**INGREDIENTS** *Makes 12 biscuits*

100g/4oz butter
50g/2oz dark brown soft sugar
100g/4oz plain flour, plus extra for dusting
50g/2oz cornflour
1 tsp ground ginger

FOR THE ICING

100g/4oz icing sugar, sifted
1 tbsp ginger syrup from a stem ginger jar
2 balls of stem ginger, chopped or grated

**METHOD**

**1.** Heat the oven to 160°C/325°F/gas 3 and grease or line a large baking sheet.
**2.** Beat the butter and sugar together until soft and creamy. Gradually work in the flour, cornflour and ginger and mix to a soft dough.
**3.** Roll out on a lightly floured surface to about 1cm/½in thick and cut into rounds with a 7.5cm/3in biscuit cutter. Prick all over with a fork and arrange on the prepared baking sheet.
**4.** Bake in the oven for about 20 minutes until pale golden brown.
**5.** Leave to cool in the tin for a few minutes, then transfer to a wire rack to finish cooling.
**6.** Mix the icing sugar and ginger syrup together and spoon over the cold biscuits. Sprinkle with the stem ginger and leave to set.

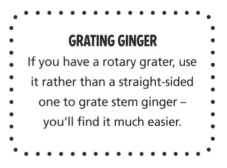

**GRATING GINGER**

If you have a rotary grater, use it rather than a straight-sided one to grate stem ginger – you'll find it much easier.

# Custard Creams

❉ ❉ ❉ ❉ ❉ ❉ ❉ ❉

*Your version of custard creams may not boast the precisely stamped cow on the side that bought ones have but they will be delicious. These are quite large biscuits.*

**INGREDIENTS** *Makes 12 biscuits*

175g/6oz butter
50g/2oz icing sugar, sifted
50g/2oz custard powder
225g/8oz plain flour, plus extra
   for dusting
FOR THE FILLING
50g/2oz butter
100g/4oz icing sugar, sifted
2 tbsp custard powder
½ tsp vanilla extract

**CHILDREN'S BAKING SETS**
You can buy children's sets of biscuit cutters with lots of different shapes and sizes and they are great fun.
There's no reason why you should make all the biscuits in a batch the same shape.

**METHOD**

**1.** Heat the oven to 160°C/325°F/ gas 3 and grease or line a large baking sheet.
**2.** Put all the ingredients in a large bowl and beat to a smooth dough.
**3.** Roll out on a lightly floured surface to about 5mm/¼in thick and cut into rectangles. Arrange on the prepared baking sheet.

**4.** Bake in the oven for about 20 minutes until pale golden.
**5.** Leave to cool on the baking sheet for 1 minute, then transfer to a wire rack to finish cooling.
**6.** Meanwhile, beat together the filling ingredients. When the biscuits are cool, use the filling to sandwich them in pairs.

# Jaffa Cakes

❀ ❀ ❀ ❀ ❀ ❀ ❀

*Layers of biscuit, orange jelly and chocolate make up these unique and distinctive biscuits. Allow yourself a little time for this recipe.*

**INGREDIENTS** *Makes 12 cakes*

½ sachet orange jelly
75ml/2½fl oz boiling water
1 egg
50g/2oz caster sugar
15g/½oz butter, melted and cooled
60g/2½oz plain flour
25g/1oz ground almonds
75g/3oz milk or dark chocolate

**METHOD**

**1.** Dissolve the jelly powder in the boiling water, then top up to 150m/¼pt with cold water. Leave to cool and begin to set, stirring occasionally.

**2.** Heat the oven to 200°C/400°F/ gas 6 and place paper cases in a 12-hole muffin tin.

**3.** Beat the egg and sugar together until light and fluffy. Add the butter, then fold in the flour and almonds. Spoon the mixture into the prepared paper cases.

**4.** Bake in the oven for 10 minutes until golden brown. Transfer to a wire rack to cool.

**5.** When the jelly is just setting, spoon it over the cold cakes. Leave to set.

**6.** Melt the chocolate in a heatproof bowl set over a pan of gently simmering water. Spoon over the top and leave to solidify.

# Iced Party Rings

*These biscuits derive their name from their popularity at children's parties. The glacé icing can be used on any plain biscuits.*

**INGREDIENTS** *Makes 15 biscuits*

250g/9oz plain flour, plus extra for sprinkling
200g/7oz butter
75g/3oz caster sugar
1 egg, lightly beaten
1 tsp vanilla extract
grated zest of ½ lemon

FOR THE ICING

100g/4oz icing sugar, sifted
1 tbsp boiling water
a few drops of food colouring

## METHOD

**1.** Heat the oven to 160°C/325°F/gas 3 and grease or line two baking sheets.

**2.** Put the flour in a bowl and rub in the butter until the mixture resembles coarse breadcrumbs, then stir in the sugar. Add the egg, vanilla and lemon zest and mix to a firm dough.

**3.** Roll out the dough on a lightly floured surface to 5mm/¼in thick and cut into 15 rounds with a 7.5cm/3in biscuit cutter. Use a petit four or shape cutter to take a circle out of the centre of the biscuits. Reroll the dough as necessary. Arrange the biscuits on the prepared baking sheet.

**4.** Bake in the oven for 12 minutes until golden brown round the edges.

**5.** Leave to cool on the baking sheet for 1 minute, then transfer to a wire rack to finish cooling.

**6.** Put the icing sugar in a small bowl and mix in the water to create a smooth icing. Smooth most of the icing over the biscuits, using a palette knife dipped in boiling water.

**7.** Colour the remaining icing with a few drops of colour, adding a little more icing sugar, if necessary. Dip a fork into the coloured icing and drag across the biscuits to create a pattern. Leave to set.

# Easter Biscuits

✱ ✱ ✱ ✱ ✱ ✱ ✱ ✱

*It won't surprise you that these are traditionally served
in spring to celebrate the end of the austerity of Lent,
when Christians give up rich foods.*

**INGREDIENTS** *Makes 12 biscuits*
75g/3oz butter
100g/4oz caster sugar
1 egg yolk
150g /5oz plain flour, plus extra
   for sprinkling
1 tsp baking powder
40g/1½oz currants
1 tsp mixed spice
about 1 tbsp milk
25g/1oz demerara sugar

**METHOD**
**1.** Heat the oven to 180°C/350°F/
gas 4 and grease and line a large
baking sheet.
**2.** Beat together the butter and
sugar until pale and creamy. Beat in
the egg yolk, then work in the flour,
baking powder, currants and mixed
spice, with enough of the milk to
make a firm dough.

**3.** Roll out on a lightly floured
surface to about 5mm/¼in thick
and cut into rounds with a 5cm/2in
biscuit cutter. Place on the prepared
baking sheet and prick with a fork.
Sprinkle with the demerara sugar.
**4.** Bake in the oven for 20 minutes
until darker round the edges.
**5.** Leave to cool on the baking sheet
for 1 minute, then transfer to a wire
rack to finish cooling.

# Ginger Crunch Biscuits

*These deliciously crunchy ginger biscuits also work well sandwiched in pairs with buttercream. Ginger is such a warming spice, and I always think of these as winter biscuits.*

**INGREDIENTS** *Makes 12 biscuits*

100g/4oz butter
50g/2oz light brown soft sugar
100g/4oz plain flour, plus extra for
    dusting
1 tsp baking powder
1 tsp ground ginger

**METHOD**

**1.** Heat the oven to 180°C/350°F/ gas 4 and grease two baking sheets.
**2.** Beat the butter and sugar together until pale and creamy. Beat in the flour, baking powder and ginger and mix to a firm dough.
**3.** Roll out on a lightly floured surface to about 5mm/¼in thick and cut into rounds with a 7.5cm/3in plain biscuit cutter. Place on the prepared baking sheet and prick with a fork.
**4.** Bake in the oven for 20 minutes until pale gold.
**5.** Leave to cool on the baking sheet for 1 minute, then transfer to a wire rack to finish cooling.

# Amaretti

*Quintessentially Italian biscuits to serve with your after-dinner espresso, amaretti are designed especially for dunking. They are really light and crunchy as they are made with egg whites.*

**INGREDIENTS** *Makes 18 biscuits*
2 egg whites
75g/3oz ground almonds
225g/8oz icing sugar

**METHOD**
**1.** Heat the oven to 180°C/350°F/
gas 4 and grease or line two
baking sheets.
**2.** Beat the egg whites until stiff.
**3.** Mix the ground almonds and
icing sugar together, then fold in
the egg whites. Spoon the mixture
into a piping bag and pipe small
circles or rings onto the prepared
baking sheet.
**4.** Bake in the oven for about
20 minutes until golden brown.
**5.** Leave to cool on the baking sheet
for 1 minute, then transfer to a wire
rack to finish cooling.

# Fig Rolls

❊ ❊ ❊ ❊ ❊ ❊ ❊

*There can't be anyone reading this who doesn't know about fig rolls – and either loves them or hates them! They are the Marmite of the biscuit world.*

**INGREDIENTS** *Makes 12 rolls*

175g/6oz dried figs, stems trimmed
   off and flesh chopped
200ml/7fl oz water
100g/4oz wholemeal flour
100g/4oz plain flour, plus extra
   for dusting
a pinch of salt
100g/4oz butter
45g/1¾oz light brown soft sugar
60–75ml/2–2½fl oz milk

**METHOD**

**1.** Heat the oven to 190°C/375°F/ gas 5 and grease or line a large baking sheet.
**2.** Put the figs and water in a small pan and bring to the boil. Reduce the heat and leave to simmer for 20 minutes, stirring occasionally, until the mixture is thick and soft. Leave to cool slightly, then drain off any excess water and purée the figs in a blender or food processor.
**3.** Put the flours and salt in a bowl. Rub in the butter until the mixture resembles coarse breadcrumbs. Stir in the sugar. Gradually add the milk and mix to a firm dough.
**4.** Divide in half and roll out each half on a lightly floured surface to about 33×6cm/13×2½in). Spread the fig purée down the centre of the length of the rectangles. Fold in the sides, dampen the edges and overlap slightly to seal together. Cut into 3cm/1¼in slices and arrange, folded-side down, on the prepared baking sheet.
**5.** Bake in the oven for 25 minutes until golden brown.
**6.** Leave to cool on the baking sheet for 1 minute, then transfer to a wire rack to finish cooling.

# Hazelnut Macaroons

*Great for a treat and certainly not for dunking, this is where 'biscuit' strays into 'cake'. The paper will stick to the bottom of the macaroons but you can simply eat it with the cake.*

**INGREDIENTS**

*Makes 12 macaroons*

2 egg whites
150g/5oz caster sugar
a few drops of vanilla extract
150g/5oz ground hazelnuts
12 hazelnuts

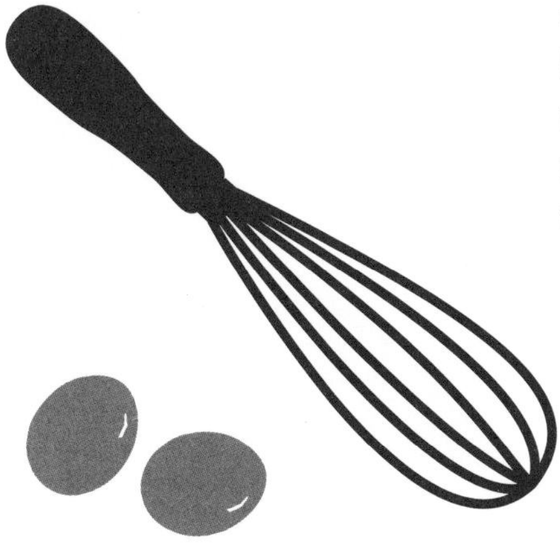

**METHOD**

**1.** Heat the oven to 190°C/375°F/gas 5. Grease a large baking sheet and line with rice paper.

**2.** Whisk the egg whites until frothy. Stir in the sugar, vanilla and nuts and mix to a paste.

**3.** Roll into 12 balls and place on the rice paper. Gently press a hazelnut into the top of each one.

**4.** Bake in the oven for 20 minutes until pale golden.

**5.** Leave to cool on the baking sheet for 5 minutes, then tear round the rice paper and transfer to a wire rack to finish cooling.

# Melting Moments

✳ ✳ ✳ ✳ ✳ ✳ ✳ ✳

*These neat little melt-in-the-mouth offerings are halfway between a cake and a biscuit, small and round but slightly soft.*

**INGREDIENTS** *Makes 18 biscuits*
50g/2oz vegetable fat or lard
50g/2oz butter
75g/3oz caster sugar
½ egg, beaten
a few drops of vanilla extract
150g/5oz plain flour
1 tsp baking powder
4 tbsp rolled oats
20 glacé cherries, halved

**METHOD**
**1.** Heat the oven to 180°C/350°F/ gas 4 and grease two baking sheets.
**2.** Beat the vegetable fat, butter and sugar together until pale and creamy. Beat in the egg and vanilla extract, then gently stir in the flour and baking powder until you have a soft dough.
**3.** Using wet hands to stop the mixture sticking to them, roll the mixture into 18 small balls. Put the oats in a shallow dish and roll the balls in the oats to coat them, then arrange them on the prepared baking sheets, allowing space between. Press a glacé cherry half into the top of each one.
**4.** Bake in the oven for 20 minutes until pale golden brown.
**5.** Leave to cool on the tray for a minute, then use a palette knife to loosen them from the tray. Leave to cool for a further few minutes, then transfer to a wire rack to cool completely.

# Almond Biscotti

❋ ❋ ❋ ❋ ❋ ❋ ❋ ❋

*These traditional Italian biscuits are baked twice to make them extra crisp. They are designed especially for dunking.*

**INGREDIENTS** *Makes 12 biscuits*

100g/4oz almonds
100g/4oz plain flour
50g/2oz caster sugar
a pinch of salt
a pinch of bicarbonate of soda
1 egg, separated
a few drops of vanilla extract

**METHOD**

**1.** Heat the oven to 180°C/350°F/ gas 4 and grease or line a large baking sheet.

**2.** Chop half the almonds and grind the other half.

**3.** Put the flour, sugar, salt and bicarbonate of soda in a bowl and mix them together. Add the chopped and ground almonds. Beat in the egg yolk and vanilla extract.

**4.** Whisk the egg white until stiff, then fold into the mixture using a metal spoon. Shape into 2 rolls

about 2.5cm/1in in diameter and place on the prepared baking sheet.

**5.** Bake in the oven for about 15 minutes until risen and pale golden brown.

**6.** Cut into 2.5cm/1in slices, return them to the baking sheet and bake for a further 10 minutes until crisp.

**7.** Leave to cool on the baking sheet for 1 minute, then transfer to a wire rack to finish cooling.

# Cantucci

✳ ✳ ✳ ✳ ✳ ✳ ✳ ✳

*The double-baking makes these Italian biscuits very crisp and therefore ideal for dipping into hot, strong coffee.*

**INGREDIENTS** *Makes 10 biscuits*
175g/6oz caster sugar
1 egg
1 egg yolk
225g/8oz plain flour
½ tsp baking powder
25g/1oz butter, melted
grated zest of ½ orange
125g/4½oz almonds, halved
   or quartered

**METHOD**
**1.** Heat the oven to 190°C/375°F/ gas 5 and grease or line two baking sheets.
**2.** Put the sugar, whole egg and egg yolk in a bowl and beat until pale and creamy. Gradually work in the flour, baking powder, butter, orange zest and almonds and mix to a soft dough. Divide in half, shape into 2 long sausages and place on one of the prepared baking sheets.

**3.** Bake in the oven for 30 minutes until pale golden brown. Remove from the oven and put to one side to cool slightly. Reduce the oven temperature to 110°C/225°F/gas ¼. Cut the cantucci into 2cm/¾in thick slices on the diagonal, and arrange them flat on two baking sheets. Return to the oven for a further 10 minutes.
**5.** Leave to cool on the baking sheets for 1 minute, then transfer to a wire rack to finish cooling.

# Sponge Fingers

✳ ✳ ✳ ✳ ✳ ✳ ✳ ✳

*These are very easy to find in the shops, but making your own will give you so much more satisfaction. The lightness comes from the whisked egg whites.*

## INGREDIENTS ❄

*Makes 18 sponge fingers*
3 eggs, separated
125g/4½oz caster sugar
100g/4oz plain flour

## METHOD

**1.** Heat the oven to 160°C/325°F/ gas 3 and grease or line two baking sheets.

**2.** Whisk the egg yolks and 100g/ 4oz of the sugar together until pale and thick. Gently fold in the flour.

**3.** Whisk the egg whites until stiff, then fold into the egg yolk mixture.

**4.** Spoon the mixture into a piping bag with a large plain nozzle and pipe biscuits about 10cm/4in long, spaced slightly apart, on the prepared baking sheets. Sprinkle with the remaining sugar.

**5.** Bake in the oven for 15 minutes until pale golden.

**6.** Leave to cool on the baking sheet for 1 minute, then transfer to a wire rack to finish cooling.

# Shredded Wheat Biscuits

✻ ✻ ✻ ✻ ✻ ✻ ✻ ✻

*These are substantial, crunchy biscuits, great for elevenses as they will certainly keep the hunger pangs away until lunch time.*

**INGREDIENTS** *Makes 12 biscuits*

225g/8oz plain flour
1 tsp bicarbonate of soda
1 tsp baking powder
a pinch of salt
1 tsp ground cinnamon
225g/8oz butter, softened
100g/4oz rolled oats
400g/14oz Shredded Wheat, crushed
250g/9oz raisins
2 eggs, lightly beaten
2 tsp vanilla extract
1 tbsp milk (optional)

**METHOD**
**1.** Heat the oven to 200°C/400°F/ gas 6 and grease or line a large baking sheet.
**2.** Mix the flour, bicarbonate of soda, baking powder, salt and cinnamon in a bowl. Rub in the butter until the mixture resembles coarse breadcrumbs. Stir in the oats, Shredded Wheat and raisins.
**3.** Gradually work in the eggs and vanilla until the mixture binds together. Add the milk, if necessary, to bind.
**4.** Shape the mixture into balls, flatten slightly and arrange on the prepared baking sheet.
**5.** Bake in the oven for about 15 minutes until golden brown.
**6.** Leave to cool on the baking sheet for 1 minute, then transfer to a wire rack to finish cooling.

# Carrot Cookies

❄ ❄ ❄ ❄ ❄ ❄ ❄ ❄

*A bit like whoopie pies, these are a biscuit version of carrot cake. If you have a food processor, that will make short work of grating the carrots.*

**INGREDIENTS** *Makes 12 cookies*

100g/4oz butter
225g/8oz dark brown soft sugar
2 eggs, lightly beaten
225g/8oz carrots, grated
225g/8oz plain flour
½ tsp bicarbonate of soda
2 tsp ground cinnamon
2 tbsp chopped mixed nuts

**FOR THE FILLING**

75g/3oz cream cheese
175g/6oz icing sugar, sifted

**METHOD**

**1.** Heat the oven to 200°C/400°F/ gas 6 and grease or line two baking sheets.
**2.** Beat the butter and sugar together until smooth and creamy. Gradually beat in the eggs, then fold in the carrots and remaining ingredients. Place spoonfuls of the mixture slightly apart on the prepared baking sheets.
**3.** Bake in the oven for about 15 minutes until risen and golden brown.
**4.** Leave to cool on the baking sheet for 1 minute, then transfer to a wire rack to finish cooling.
**5.** Beat the cheese and icing sugar together until smooth, then sandwich the biscuits in pairs.

# Jumbles

*This is a really traditional recipe for a soft, slightly cakey biscuit (or perhaps biscuity cake) with a delicious, crunchy sugar coating. Use demerara sugar for an even crunchier effect.*

## INGREDIENTS

*Makes about 12 biscuits*

50g/2oz butter
50g/2oz light brown soft sugar
100g/4oz self-raising flour,
  plus extra for dusting
1 egg, lightly beaten
about 12 almonds

FOR THE COATING

30g/1oz light brown soft sugar
15g/½oz plain flour
1 tsp ground cinnamon

## METHOD

**1.** Heat the oven to 180°C/350°F/gas 4 and grease or line two baking sheets.

**2.** Beat the butter and sugar together until pale and creamy. Gradually work in the flour and about half the beaten egg to make a stiff dough. Divide into 12 pieces.

**3.** To make the coating, put the sugar, flour and cinnamon in a bowl and mix together.

**4.** Dust your hands with flour and roll out the dough pieces into sausage shapes about 1cm/½in thick. Roll in the sugar mixture. Moisten the ends with some of the remaining egg and seal them into a ring. Place on the prepared baking sheets and press an almond into each one.

**5.** Bake in the oven for 15–20 minutes until golden. Transfer to a wire rack to cool.

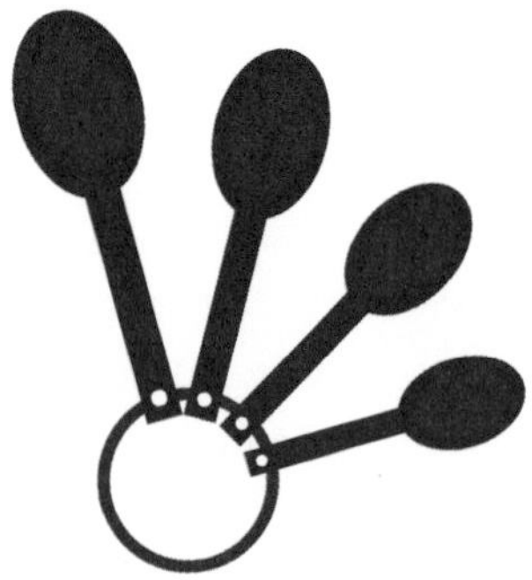

# Lemon Puffs

✳ ✳ ✳ ✳ ✳ ✳ ✳ ✳

*Shiny puff pastry encasing a lemon curd filling – these have to be eaten quickly or they will go soggy, which is a good excuse to polish them off. Use jam and cream for the filling if you prefer.*

## INGREDIENTS

*Makes 12 biscuits*
375g/13oz ready-rolled puff pastry
50g/2oz icing sugar, sifted

### FOR THE FILLING
75g/3oz lemon curd
50g/2oz icing sugar, sifted

## METHOD

**1.** Heat the oven to 200°C/400°F/ gas 6 and grease or line two baking sheets.

**2.** Unroll the pastry on to its baking paper wrap. Cut into 24 equal rectangles and sprinkle generously with icing sugar. Transfer to the prepared baking sheets.

**3.** Bake in the oven for 15 minutes until well risen and golden on top.

**4.** Leave to cool on the baking sheet for 1 minute, then transfer to a wire rack to finish cooling.

**5.** Beat the lemon curd and icing sugar together and use it to sandwich pairs of biscuits, with the shiny side on the outside.

# Indian Semolina Biscuits

✻ ✻ ✻ ✻ ✻ ✻ ✻ ✻

*This recipe makes nice small, round biscuits that are ideal for children.
I have given weights here, but if you prefer to use the quick cup
measures, follow the quantities in the box.*

## INGREDIENTS
*Makes 20 small biscuits*
100g/4oz plain flour
125g/4½oz semolina
150g/5oz caster sugar
75g/3oz gram flour
175g/6oz ghee (clarified butter)

## METHOD
**1.** Heat the oven to 150°C/300°F/
gas 2. Grease two baking sheets and
line them with baking paper.
**2.** Mix all the dry ingredients in a
bowl, then rub in the ghee and
mould the mixture with the palms of
your hands until it begins to form a
fairly stiff dough. You may need to
add a little more ghee.
**3.** Shape into balls, gently press
slightly flatter, then arrange on the
prepared baking sheets.
**4.** Bake in the oven for 30 minutes

until lightly browned, with hairline
cracks across the surface.
**5.** Leave to cool on the baking sheet
for 1 minute, then transfer to a wire
rack to finish cooling.

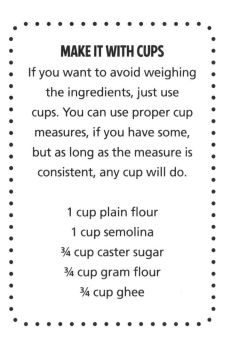

### MAKE IT WITH CUPS
If you want to avoid weighing
the ingredients, just use
cups. You can use proper cup
measures, if you have some,
but as long as the measure is
consistent, any cup will do.

1 cup plain flour
1 cup semolina
¾ cup caster sugar
¾ cup gram flour
¾ cup ghee

# CHAPTER 6

✻✻✻✻✻✻✻✻

# COOKIES & WHOOPIE PIES

In the UK, the term 'cookies' is generally reserved for something bigger and more substantial than a biscuit. In the USA, it replaces what the Brits mean by the word 'biscuit'. It's a bit like the fact that a sandwich cake is almost always round but a flapjack is usually square – it doesn't always make a lot of sense, but we like to stick to our definitions. As for 'whoopie pies' – well, that's just bizarre!

# Is it a biscuit or a cookie?

✳ ✳ ✳ ✳ ✳ ✳ ✳ ✳

**W**hat you call that small baked object on your plate really depends upon your linguistic and culinary heritage. Of course, what matters most is how good it tastes, whatever its name may be!

The English word 'biscuit' stems from the Latin *bis coctus*, meaning 'twice baked', and was applied to the hard biscuits that were part of army rations. As the variety of biscuits expanded, the name remained and came to describe any kind of small, thin, flat cake made principally of flour and milk, usually but not always sweet, and flavoured with a whole selection of other ingredients.

'Cookie', on the other hand, derives from the Dutch word *'koekjes'*, meaning small cake. Introduced to the US with the immigrant population, it became anglicized and absorbed into the vernacular as the term most used in the United States.

Invented in the 1920s, supposedly by the American Amish communities in Maine, whoopie pies are halfway to being a cake rather than a biscuit. On seeing these treats on the table, children are said to have cried out, 'Whoopie!'

At the end of the day, it really doesn't make a lot of difference whether it's a cookie or a biscuit, a cake or a pie! For the purposes of this chapter, my definition groups the larger and more impressive offerings together. Just as a muffin is usually bigger than a cupcake, here are some deliciously indulgent and impressively big biscuits – or cookies.

# Giant Chocolate Chunk Cookies

✳ ✳ ✳ ✳ ✳ ✳ ✳ ✳

*Of course, you don't have to make these into giant cookies – but saying that the recipe insisted on maximum size is a great excuse.*

## INGREDIENTS

*Makes 6 large cookies*
100g/4oz butter
100g/4oz caster sugar
75g/3oz dark brown soft sugar
½ tsp vanilla extract
1 egg, lightly beaten
125g/4½oz plain flour, plus extra
    for dusting
¼ tsp bicarbonate of soda
1 tbsp cocoa powder
100g/4oz dark chocolate,
    cut into chunks
100g/4oz milk chocolate,
    cut into chunks

## METHOD

**1.** Heat the oven to 190°C/375°F/ gas 5 and grease or line a large baking sheet.
**2.** Put the butter and sugars in a bowl and beat until pale and creamy. Add the vanilla to the egg and gradually work in alternately with spoonfuls of the flour, bicarbonate of soda, cocoa and chocolate chunks, mixing to a soft dough.
**3.** Shape into balls with lightly floured hands, flatten slightly, and arrange well apart on the prepared baking sheet.
**4.** Bake in the oven for 10 minutes until darker around the edges.
**5.** Leave to cool on the baking sheet for 1 minute, then transfer to a wire rack to finish cooling.

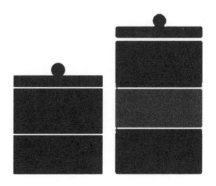

# Oat & Sultana Cookies

❋ ❋ ❋ ❋ ❋ ❋ ❋ ❋

*Not only do oats taste great and have a fabulous texture, they are good for you, too. That makes these cookies a win-win option.*

## INGREDIENTS *Makes 12 cookies*

50g/2oz butter
150g/5oz canned caramel
2 tbsp cream or milk
100g/4oz plain flour, plus extra
  for dusting
100g/4oz rolled oats
½ tsp baking powder

## METHOD

**1.** Heat the oven to 180°C/350°F/gas 4 and grease or line two baking sheets.

**2.** Put the butter, caramel and cream or milk in a large bowl and beat until soft. Beat in the flour, oats and baking powder and mix to a soft dough.

**3.** Shape into small balls with lightly floured hands, flatten slightly, and arrange well apart on the prepared baking sheets.

**4.** Bake in the oven for about 10 minutes until slightly darker around the edges.

**5.** Leave to cool on the baking sheets for 1 minute, then transfer to a wire rack to finish cooling.

# Butterscotch & Pecan Cookies

✳ ✳ ✳ ✳ ✳ ✳ ✳ ✳

*Pecan nuts have a lovely soft texture that makes them ideal for cookies.
If you like, you can top each biscuit with a pecan half.*

**INGREDIENTS** *Makes 12 cookies*
50g/2oz butter
150g/5oz dark brown soft sugar
2 tbsp milk
1 tsp vanilla
100g/4oz plain flour
1 tbsp cornflour
½ tsp baking powder
25g/1oz pecan nuts, chopped
50g/2oz chocolate chips

**METHOD**
**1.** Heat the oven to 180°C/350°F/ gas 4 and grease or line two baking sheets.
**2.** Melt the butter and sugar in a small pan over a low heat.
**3.** Remove from the heat and add the remaining ingredients, mixing to a soft dough. Shape spoonfuls of the mixture well apart on the prepared baking sheets.
**4.** Bake in the oven for about 10 minutes until darker around the edges.
**5.** Leave to cool on the baking sheet for 1 minute, then transfer to a wire rack to finish cooling.

**EAT SOME, FREEZE SOME**
If you keep a few biscuits in the freezer, they make a handy snack at a moment's notice.

# Spotted Nut & White Chocolate Cookies

❋ ❋ ❋ ❋ ❋ ❋ ❋ ❋

*People either love white chocolate or hate it – it is very sweet, so a little goes a long way. For those who love it, here is a mega cookie with white chocolate chips.*

## INGREDIENTS

*Makes 12 large cookies*
225g/8oz butter, softened
225g/8oz caster sugar
225g/8oz light brown soft sugar
3 eggs, lightly beaten
2 tsp vanilla extract
225g/8oz plain flour
1 tsp baking powder
1 tsp bicarbonate of soda
225g/8oz rolled oats
100g/4oz desiccated coconut
100g/4oz pecan nuts, chopped
50g/2oz white chocolate chips

## METHOD

**1.** Heat the oven to 180°C/350°F/gas 4 and grease two baking sheets.
**2.** Put the butter and sugar in a large bowl and beat until pale and creamy. Gradually beat in the eggs and vanilla alternately with spoonfuls of the flour, baking powder and bicarbonate of soda, then add the remaining ingredients and mix to a fairly stiff dough.
**3.** Shape into balls and arrange well apart on the prepared baking sheets.
**4.** Bake in the oven for 15 minutes until golden brown.
**5.** Leave to cool on the baking sheets, then transfer to a wire rack to finish cooling.

### CHOOSE YOUR CHOCOLATE
You can use whichever type of chocolate chip or chunk you prefer for this recipe, or just chop up a bar of chocolate.

# Rye Flake Cookies

✳ ✳ ✳ ✳ ✳ ✳ ✳ ✳

*You may need to go to a health food store to find rye flakes, though they are also on sale in some major supermarkets.*

**INGREDIENTS** *Makes 12 cookies*

75g/3oz wholemeal flour,
   plus extra for dusting
175g/6oz rye flakes
½ tsp baking powder
150g/5oz sugar
50g/2oz dates, chopped
2 tbsp agave syrup
½ tsp vanilla extract
4 tbsp coconut oil
4 tbsp apple sauce

**METHOD**

**1.** Heat the oven to 180°C/350°F/ gas 4 and grease or line two baking sheets.
**2.** Stir the dry ingredients and the dates together, then stir in the remaining ingredients and mix to a smooth dough.
**3.** Shape into small balls with lightly floured hands, flatten slightly, and arrange well apart on the prepared baking sheets.
**4.** Bake in the oven for about 15 minutes until golden brown.
**5.** Leave to cool on the baking sheet for 1 minute, then transfer to a wire rack to finish cooling.

# Banana Chip & Honey Cookies

✻ ✻ ✻ ✻ ✻ ✻ ✻ ✻

*You could also make these cookies with maple syrup instead of honey for its distinctive flavour. The banana chips give them a pleasing crunchiness.*

**INGREDIENTS** *Makes 12 cookies*
50g/2oz butter
150g/5oz clear honey
2 tbsp milk
100g/4oz plain flour
½ tsp baking powder
75g/3oz banana chips

**METHOD**
**1.** Heat the oven to 180°C/350°F/gas 4 and grease or line two baking sheets.

**2.** Put the butter and honey in a bowl and beat until blended, then gradually work in the remaining ingredients to make a soft dough.

**3.** Place spoonfuls of the mixture well apart on the baking sheets.

**4.** Bake in the oven for about 10 minutes until light golden brown.

**5.** Leave to cool on the baking sheet for 1 minute, then transfer to a wire rack to finish cooling.

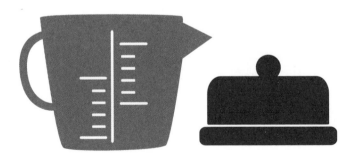

# Lemon & Lavender Cookies

✱ ✱ ✱ ✱ ✱ ✱ ✱ ✱

*Use culinary lavender flowers from a cookshop, or buy them from an online source. Omit the lavender to make plain lemon cookies.*

## INGREDIENTS *Makes 12 cookies*

100g/4oz butter
175g/6oz light brown soft sugar
grated zest of 2 lemons
175g/6oz plain flour
2 tsp cornflour
1 tsp baking powder
2 tbsp milk
2 tbsp lavender flowers

## METHOD

**1.** Heat the oven to 180°C/350°F/gas 4 and grease or line two baking sheets.

**2.** Put the butter and sugar in a large bowl and beat until light and creamy. Gradually work in the lemon zest, flour, cornflour, baking powder, milk and lavender and mix to a soft dough. Shape spoonfuls well apart on the prepared baking sheets.

**3.** Bake in the oven for about 15 minutes until golden.

**4.** Leave to cool on the baking sheet for 1 minute, then transfer to a wire rack to finish cooling.

# Nutty Cookies

✳ ✳ ✳ ✳ ✳ ✳ ✳ ✳

*These are mixed-nut cookies, golden brown and chocolate chipped.
You can use dark, milk or white chocolate. If you don't have chips,
just chop up a bar.*

**INGREDIENTS** *Makes 12 cookies*
150g/5oz butter
125g/5oz dark brown soft sugar
1 egg, lightly beaten
1 tsp vanilla extract
175g/6oz plain flour
½ tsp bicarbonate of soda
100g/4oz chocolate chips
100g/4oz chopped mixed nuts

**METHOD**
**1.** Heat the oven to 180°C/350°F/
gas 4 and grease or line two
baking sheets.
**2.** Put the butter and sugar in a large
bowl and beat until pale and creamy.
Beat in the egg, then fold in the
remaining ingredients and mix to a
soft dough.
**3.** Place spoonfuls of the mixture
well apart on the baking sheets.

**4.** Bake in the oven for about
15 minutes until golden brown.
**5.** Leave to cool on the baking sheets
for 1 minute, then transfer to a wire
rack to finish cooling.

# Cranberry Cookies

❋ ❋ ❋ ❋ ❋ ❋ ❋ ❋

*A packet of dried cranberries is a handy item to keep in the storecupboard to liven up simple biscuits and make them a bit more unusual than biscuits with raisins.*

**INGREDIENTS** *Makes 12 cookies*
50g/2oz butter
50g/2oz light brown soft sugar
grated zest of 1 orange
1 tsp orange juice
50g/2oz plain flour, plus extra
    for dusting
½ tsp bicarbonate of soda
50g/2oz dried cranberries
1 tbsp chopped walnuts

**METHOD**
**1.** Heat the oven to 180°C/350°F/ gas 4 and grease or line a large baking sheet.
**2.** Put the butter, sugar and orange zest in a bowl and beat until pale and creamy. Gradually mix in the remaining ingredients to make a soft dough.
**3.** Roll out on a lightly floured surface to about 5mm/¼in thick and cut into rounds with a 7.5cm/3in biscuit cutter. Arrange on the prepared baking sheet.
**4.** Bake in the oven for about 12 minutes until golden brown.
**5.** Leave to cool on the baking sheet for 1 minute, then transfer to a wire rack to finish cooling.

# Gingerbread Men

❋ ❋ ❋ ❋ ❋ ❋ ❋ ❋

*These are not just for kids – people of all ages love gingerbread men, so grab your gingerbread man cutter and have fun with this traditional recipe.*

**INGREDIENTS** *Makes 12 men*

350g/12oz plain flour, plus extra
 for dusting
1 tsp bicarbonate of soda
2 tsp ground ginger
100g/4oz butter
175g/6oz light brown soft sugar
1 egg, lightly beaten
4 tbsp golden syrup

**TO DECORATE**

a few currants
1–2 tsp hot water (optional)
2 tbsp icing sugar, sifted (optional)

**METHOD**

**1.** Heat the oven to 190°C/375°F/ gas 5 and grease or line two baking sheets.

**2.** Put the flour, bicarbonate of soda and ginger in a bowl. Rub in the butter until the mixture resembles coarse breadcrumbs, then stir in the sugar. Make a well in the centre and add the egg and syrup. Mix all the ingredients to a smooth dough.

**3.** Roll out on a lightly floured surface to about 5mm/¼in thick and cut into shapes with a gingerbread man cutter. Arrange on the prepared baking sheets.

**4.** Traditionally, gingerbread men have only eyes and buttons, so gently press the currants into the dough to represent these.

**5.** Bake in the oven for 15 minutes until darker around the edges. Leave

to cool on the baking sheet for 1 minute, then transfer to a wire rack to finish cooling.

**6.** If you wish to decorate the gingerbread men further, mix the hot water into the icing sugar a drop at a time until you have a smooth icing.

**7.** Use a piping bag with a very fine nozzle to make lines of icing over the biscuits to represent clothes or features, or to simply drizzle the icing. Leave to set.

### JAZZY GINGERBREAD

You can also use glacé icing, tubes of ready-made piping icing, sugar-coated sweets, jelly sweets, and liquorice strands. Go to town on your embellishments and make some really jazzy gingerbread men.

# Blueberry Cookies

✽ ✽ ✽ ✽ ✽ ✽ ✽ ✽

*Thick, chunky and delicious cookies for any occasion, these have dark brown soft sugar to give a more treacly flavour and gooey texture.*

**INGREDIENTS** *Makes 12 cookies*
100g/4oz butter
100g/4oz dark brown soft sugar
75g/3oz granulated sugar
1 egg, lightly beaten
½ tsp vanilla extract
150g/5oz plain flour
1 tsp bicarbonate of soda
a pinch of salt
75g/3oz blueberries

**METHOD**
**1.** Heat the oven to 190°C/375°F/ gas 5 and grease or line two baking sheets.
**2.** Put the butter and sugar in a large bowl and beat until pale and creamy. Gradually work in the egg and vanilla alternately with spoonfuls of the flour, bicarbonate of soda and salt and mix to a soft dough. Stir in the blueberries.
**3.** Place spoonfuls of the mixture well apart on the prepared baking sheets and flatten slightly.
**4.** Bake in the oven for about 15 minutes until golden brown. Leave to cool on the baking sheet for 1 minute, then transfer to a wire rack to finish cooling.

# Gingerbread Cookies

*These crisp little round biscuits are originally from the Midlands of England and are sometimes called white buttons – which is odd, since they are pale but not white.*

**INGREDIENTS** *Makes 24 biscuits*

300g/11oz caster sugar
100g/4oz butter
1 egg, lightly beaten
250g/9oz self-raising flour
1 tsp ground ginger

**METHOD**

**1.** Heat the oven to 150°C/300°F/ gas 2 and grease two baking sheets.

**2.** Beat the sugar and butter in a large bowl until creamy. Gradually beat in the egg alternately with the flour and ginger and mix to a dough. Roll into walnut-sized balls and arrange well apart on the prepared baking sheets.

**3.** Bake in the oven for 35 minutes until risen and pale gold in colour.

**4.** Leave to cool on the baking sheet for 1 minute, then transfer to a wire rack to finish cooling.

# Treacle Whoopie Pies with Raspberries

✳ ✳ ✳ ✳ ✳ ✳ ✳

*The rich, dark taste of treacle permeates this recipe, offset by the cool cream and raspberries. Assemble the pies just before you want to eat them.*

## INGREDIENTS

*Makes 12 whoopie pies*
100g/4oz plain flour
50g/2oz ground almonds
1 tsp bicarbonate of soda
½ tsp baking powder
50g/2oz butter
100g/4oz black treacle
1 egg, lightly beaten

### FOR THE FILLING

150ml/5fl oz double or
  whipping cream
50g/2oz icing sugar (optional)
100g/4oz raspberries

## METHOD

**1.** Heat the oven to 180°C/350°F/ gas 4 and grease two baking sheets.
**2.** Put the flour, ground almonds, bicarbonate of soda and baking powder in a bowl and mix together.
**3.** In a separate bowl, cream the butter and treacle together until well blended. Gradually add the egg alternately with spoonfuls of the flour mixture until everything is smooth and well blended. If possible, chill for 30 minutes.
**4.** Place 24 spoonfuls of the mixture well apart on the baking sheets.
**5.** Bake in the oven for 20 minutes until rounded in shape and springy to the touch.
**6.** Leave to cool on the baking sheets for 5 minutes, then transfer to a wire rack to finish cooling.
**7.** Whip the cream until stiff, blending in the icing sugar if liked. Divide half the cream between half the pies, top with the raspberries, then finish with the remaining cream and top with the remaining pies.

# Caramel & Cream Whoopie Pies

✳ ✳ ✳ ✳ ✳ ✳ ✳ ✳

*I like these filled with plain whipped cream – although it does mean they have to be eaten quickly otherwise they go soft. Just fill the amount you are sure will be eaten straight away.*

## INGREDIENTS

*Makes 12 whoopie pies*
225g/8oz plain flour
1½ tsp bicarbonate of soda
½ tsp mixed spice
¼ tsp salt
400g/14oz canned caramel
1 egg, lightly beaten
150ml/4fl oz milk
150ml/4fl oz sunflower oil
150ml/5fl oz double or
   whipping cream

## METHOD

**1.** Heat the oven to 180°C/350°F/ gas 4 and line two baking sheets.
**2.** Mix the flour, bicarbonate of soda, mixed spice and salt in a bowl.
**3.** In a separate bowl, beat the caramel with the egg, milk and oil. Beat the two mixtures together to form a soft dough.
**4.** Drop 24 heaped tablespoonfuls on to the prepared baking sheets, about 5cm/2in apart.
**5.** Bake in the oven for 10 minutes until springy to the touch.
**6.** Leave to cool on the baking sheet for 1 minute, then turn out onto a wire rack to finish cooling.
**7.** Whisk the cream until stiff, then sandwich the cakes together in pairs.

# Chocolate & Soured Cream Whoopie Pies

✳ ✳ ✳ ✳ ✳ ✳ ✳ ✳

*Soft and spongy like a cake, but small and shaped like a biscuit, this is a chocolate whoopie pie option.*

## INGREDIENTS

*Makes 12 whoopie pies*

25g/1oz dark chocolate,
  broken into chunks
25g/1oz butter
125g/4½oz light brown soft sugar
1 egg
½ tsp vanilla extract
100g/4oz plain flour
1 tbsp cocoa powder
½ tsp bicarbonate of soda
a pinch of ground cinnamon
a pinch of freshly grated nutmeg
120ml/4fl oz soured cream

**FOR THE FILLING**

150m/5fl oz double cream
2 tbsp cocoa powder
50g/2oz icing sugar, sifted

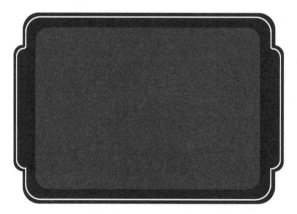

## METHOD

**1.** Heat the oven to 190°C/375°F/ gas 5 and grease or line two baking sheets.

**2.** Melt the chocolate in a heatproof bowl set over a pan of gently simmering water. Leave to one side to cool slightly.

**3.** In a large bowl, beat the butter and sugar until pale and creamy. Gradually beat in the egg and vanilla until well blended, then beat in the melted chocolate. Finally beat in the flour, cocoa, bicarbonate of soda, cinnamon, nutmeg and soured cream. Place 24 spoonfuls of the mixture well apart on the prepared baking sheets.

**4.** Bake in the oven for 15 minutes until rounded and just springy to the touch in the centre.

**5.** Leave to cool on the baking sheet for 1 minute, then transfer to a wire rack to finish cooling.

**6.** Beat the filling ingredients together and use to sandwich the cool whoopie pies in pairs.

# Carrot & Cream Cheese Whoopie Pies

✳ ✳ ✳ ✳ ✳ ✳ ✳ ✳

*Unlike most smooth and rounded whoopie pies, these are a little rustic as the grated carrot makes them a bit more lumpy.*

## INGREDIENTS

*Makes 12 whoopie pies*
100g/4oz plain flour
1 tsp bicarbonate of soda
½ tsp baking powder
1 tsp ground cinnamon
a pinch of ground ginger
50g/2oz butter
100g/4oz light brown soft sugar
1 egg, lightly beaten
½ tsp vanilla extract
2 carrots, grated
50g/2oz pecan nuts, chopped

### FOR THE FILLING

100g/4oz icing sugar
75g/3oz cream cheese
grated zest of ½ lemon
50g/2oz butter
1 tsp orange juice

## METHOD

**1.** Heat the oven to 180°C/350°F/ gas 4 and grease or line two baking sheets.

**2.** Put the flour, bicarbonate of soda, baking powder, cinnamon and ginger in a bowl and mix together.

**3.** In a separate bowl, cream together the butter and sugar until light and creamy. Gradually add the egg and vanilla, beating all the time, then mix in the dry ingredients followed by the carrots and pecans. If possible, chill for 30 minutes.

**4.** Place 24 spoonfuls of the mixture well apart on the prepared baking sheets.

**5.** Bake in the oven for 20 minutes until rounded in shape and springy to the touch.

**6.** Leave to cool on the baking sheet for 5 minutes, then transfer to a wire rack to finish cooling.

**7.** To make the icing, mix all the ingredients together until well blended and smooth. Use to sandwich the pies in pairs.

# Mint Chocolate Whoopie Pies

✳ ✳ ✳ ✳ ✳ ✳ ✳ ✳

*Mint and chocolate make a common flavour combination and it works well, as always, in these whoopie pies.*

## INGREDIENTS

*Makes 12 whoopie pies*
200g/7oz plain flour
75g/3oz cocoa powder
1½ tsp bicarbonate of soda
a pinch of salt
150g/5oz butter
225g/8oz caster sugar
1 egg, lightly beaten
200ml/7fl oz milk
6 mint chocolates, chopped
**FOR THE VANILLA CREAM**
100g/4oz icing sugar
50g/2oz butter
1 tsp vanilla extract

## METHOD

**1.** Heat the oven to 190°C/375°F/ gas 5 and line two baking sheets.
**2.** Mix the flour, cocoa, bicarbonate of soda and salt in a bowl.
**3.** In a separate bowl, beat the butter and sugar until pale and creamy. Add the egg and beat for a minute or so until light and well blended. Continue beating as you add alternate spoonfuls of milk and the flour mixture until you have a soft dough. Drop 24 heaped tablespoonfuls on to the prepared baking sheets about 5cm/2in apart.
**4.** Bake in the oven for 10 minutes until springy to the touch.
**5.** Leave to cool on the baking sheet for a few minutes before turning out onto a wire rack to finish cooling.
**6.** To make the filling, beat the icing sugar with the butter and vanilla until soft. Spread over half the whoopie pies, then sandwich them together in pairs.

# CHAPTER 7

********

# SAVOURY BISCUITS

It's nice to make savoury biscuits to serve with cheese, pâté or dips, or even with your breakfast marmalade. This chapter offers a selection of both rugged, crunchy biscuits and simpler, thin, crisp options.

# Biscuits for all seasons

Savoury biscuits are popular with cheese, of course, but are also ideal with pâté or dips; to accompany a starter, salad, or soup; or just to enjoy on their own or with fresh butter.

These biscuits are often made with wholemeal flour, giving them a nuttier flavour and denser texture. Good results are also achieved using half wholemeal and half ordinary plain flour, making the final biscuit lighter. Oats often feature, as they have such a great taste and texture; we have already seen how good they taste in sweet biscuits too.

Keep your biscuits well sealed in an airtight container so that they stay fresh for longer. Biscuit tins are fine as long as the lid fits tightly. If you have been using one for some time, check that there are no dents in the tin that might have ruined the seal. Clip-top plastic boxes are good because you can be certain that they are properly airtight.

Because biscuits are so quick to make it is worth baking several different types in one go, then you can also put a few of each in the freezer and serve a variety of biscuits to your family or guests.

Finally, don't be afraid to mix sweet and savoury – it can sometimes work very well. We enjoy a slice of crumbly Wensleydale cheese with fruit cake, so why not try a plain sweet biscuit, such as a digestive, with cheese or pâté – or one of these savoury biscuits with a drizzle of honey.

# Muesli Biscuits

❋ ❋ ❋ ❋ ❋ ❋ ❋ ❋

*Perfect for breakfast, even better for the lunch box, here's a good-for-you biscuit option for cheese, pâté, soup and all kinds of other dishes.*

**INGREDIENTS** *Makes 18 biscuits*
150g/5oz butter
100g/4oz dark brown soft sugar
50g/2oz caster sugar
1 egg, lightly beaten
175g/6oz plain flour
1 tsp bicarbonate of soda
100g/4oz rolled oats
175g/6oz sultanas
1 tsp ground cinnamon

**METHOD**

**1.** Heat the oven to 160°C/325°F/ gas 3 and grease or line two baking sheets.

**2.** Put the butter and sugars in a bowl and beat until pale and creamy. Gradually work in the egg.

**3.** Mix the remaining ingredients in a separate bowl, then fold into the sugar mixture.

**4.** Roll spoonfuls of the mixture into balls and place well apart on the prepared baking sheets.

**5.** Bake in the oven for about 15 minutes until golden brown.

**6.** Leave to cool on the baking sheet for 1 minute, then transfer to a wire rack to finish cooling.

# Cheese & Tomato Twirls

✻ ✻ ✻ ✻ ✻ ✻ ✻ ✻

*Simple and quick, these are ideal for popping in the oven
if you have unexpected guests come round for drinks.*

**INGREDIENTS** *Makes 20 twirls* ❄

375g/13oz ready-rolled puff pastry
2 tbsp olive oil
3 tbsp tomato purée
salt and freshly ground black pepper
50g/2oz freshly grated Parmesan
  cheese

**METHOD**

**1.** Heat the oven to 220°C/425°F/
gas 7 and grease and line two
baking sheets.
**2.** Unroll the pastry, leaving it on
the wrapper. Brush with the oil
and spread with the tomato purée.
Season with a little salt and plenty
of pepper, then sprinkle with the
Parmesan.
**3.** Use a sharp knife or a pizza
wheel to cut the sheet across into
2.5cm/1in strips. Put one strip on the
prepared baking sheet. Holding one
end, twist the pastry into a spiral.
Repeat with the remaining pastry.
**4.** Bake in the oven for 10 minutes
until puffed up and crisp.
**5.** Serve warm or leave to cool
before serving.

# Mediterranean Herb Biscuits

✳ ✳ ✳ ✳ ✳ ✳ ✳ ✳

*An easy recipe that is reliably good, this is best with fresh herbs – but if you don't have any you can substitute dried herbs, using half the quantity.*

**INGREDIENTS** *Makes 12 biscuits*

2 sun-dried tomatoes, finely chopped
300g/11oz plain flour, plus extra
   for dusting
1 tbsp caster sugar
1 tbsp baking powder
1 garlic clove, crushed
2 tsp chopped thyme
1 tsp chopped basil
salt and freshly ground black pepper
100g/4oz butter
50g/2oz Parmesan cheese,
   freshly grated
4 tbsp yogurt
120ml/4fl oz milk

**METHOD**

**1.** Put the tomatoes in a bowl of boiling water and leave to soak while you start the biscuits.
**2.** Heat the oven to 180°C/350°F/ gas 4 and grease two baking sheets.

**3.** Put the flour, sugar, baking powder, garlic, thyme and basil in a bowl. Season with salt and pepper. Rub in the butter until the mixture resembles coarse breadcrumbs. Stir in the Parmesan, yogurt and milk and mix to a firm dough.
**4.** Roll out on a lightly floured surface to about 1cm/¾in thick and cut into rounds with a 7.5cm/3in biscuit cutter. Arrange on the prepared baking sheets.
**5.** Bake in the oven for about 12 minutes until golden brown.
**6.** Leave to cool on the baking sheet for 1 minute, then transfer to a wire rack to finish cooling.

# Crumbly Oat Thins

✳ ✳ ✳ ✳ ✳ ✳ ✳ ✳

*If you have a gluten intolerance but are able to eat oats without a problem, you can simply use gluten-free flour and baking powder in order to make this recipe suitable.*

**INGREDIENTS** *Makes 12 biscuits*

100g/4oz oatmeal
50g/2oz plain flour, plus extra
  for dusting
1 tsp baking powder
50g/2oz caster sugar
a pinch of salt
50g/2oz butter
2 tbsp milk

**METHOD**

**1.** Heat the oven to 180°C/350°F/ gas 4 and grease or line a large baking sheet.
**2.** Mix together the oats, flour, baking powder, sugar and salt. Rub in the butter until the mixture resembles breadcrumbs. Gradually add the milk and work to a firm dough.
**3.** Roll out on a lightly floured surface and cut into rounds with a 7.5cm/3cm biscuit cutter.

**4.** Place on the prepared baking sheet and bake in the oven for 15–20 minutes until light golden brown.
**5.** Leave to cool for 1 minute, then transfer to a wire rack to finish cooling.

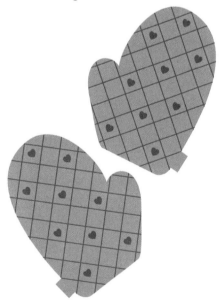

# Marmite Crackers

✳ ✳ ✳ ✳ ✳ ✳ ✳ ✳

*People either love Marmite or hate it, but even if you usually fall into
the latter category, give these crackers a try – they are great with dips.*

**INGREDIENTS** *Makes 20 biscuits*

225g/8oz plain flour, plus extra
    for dusting
50g/2oz ground almonds
1 tsp Dijon mustard
2 tbsp Marmite
2 tbsp milk
2 tbsp olive oil
2 tbsp sesame seeds

**METHOD**

**1.** Heat the oven to 200°C/400°F/
gas 6 and grease or line a large
baking sheet.

**2.** Mix the flour and almonds in a
bowl. Add the mustard, Marmite,
milk and olive oil and mix to a
firm dough.

**3.** Roll out on a lightly floured
surface to about 5mm/¼in thick
and cut out with a 5cm/2in square
biscuit cutter. Arrange on the
prepared baking sheet and sprinkle
with the sesame seeds.

**4.** Bake in the oven for 15 minutes
until browned.

**5.** Leave to cool on the baking sheet
for about 1 minute, then transfer to
a wire rack to finish cooling.

# Caraway Seed Biscuits

✾ ✾ ✾ ✾ ✾ ✾ ✾ ✾

*Sometimes called Tonbridge biscuits, these have caraway seeds
to make an interesting and distinctive topping.*

**INGREDIENTS** *Makes 12 biscuits*

225g/8oz plain flour, plus extra
   for dusting
2 tbsp caraway seeds
75g/3oz butter
75g/3oz caster sugar
1 egg, lightly beaten

**METHOD**

**1.** Heat the oven to 180°C/350°F/
gas 4 and grease or line two
baking sheets.
**2.** Put the flour and caraway seeds
in a bowl. Rub in the butter until
the mixture resembles coarse
breadcrumbs. Stir in the sugar,
then add the egg and mix to a
firm dough.
**3.** Roll out on a lightly floured
surface to about 5mm/¼in thick
and cut into rounds with a 10cm/4in
biscuit cutter. Arrange on the
prepared baking sheets.

**4.** Bake in the oven for about
10 minutes until golden brown.
**5.** Leave to cool on the baking sheets
for 1 minute, then transfer to a wire
rack to finish cooling.

# Paprika Thins

✳ ✳ ✳ ✳ ✳ ✳ ✳ ✳

*Fine oatmeal is best for these biscuits, but you could use medium oatmeal or even rolled oats and still make them successfully.*

**INGREDIENTS** *Makes 12 biscuits*
100g/4oz plain flour, plus extra
   for dusting
50g/2oz oatmeal
1 tsp paprika
1 tsp baking powder
a pinch of salt
50g/2oz butter
2 tbsp soured cream or yogurt

**METHOD**
**1.** Heat the oven to 180°C/350°F/
gas 4 and grease or line a large
baking sheet.
**2.** Mix together the flour, oatmeal,
paprika, baking powder and salt.
Rub in the butter until the mixture
resembles breadcrumbs. Gradually
add the soured cream or yogurt and
work to a firm dough.
**3.** Roll out on a lightly floured
surface and cut into rounds with a
7.5cm/3cm biscuit cutter. Place on

the prepared baking sheet.
**4.** Bake in the oven for 15–20
minutes until light golden brown.
**5.** Leave to cool on the baking sheet
for 1 minute, then transfer to a wire
rack to finish cooling.

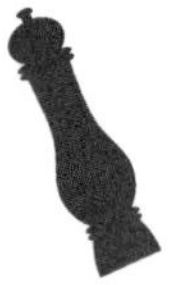

# Blue Cheese Biscuits

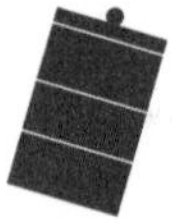

*Blue cheeses, such as Stilton, have a very distinctive and slightly salty flavour. These are quite chunky biscuits with a lovely texture created by the melting cheese.*

**INGREDIENTS** *Makes 12 biscuits*

100g/4oz Stilton cheese, crumbled
100g/4oz plain flour
freshly ground black pepper
1 egg, lightly beaten
2 tbsp poppy seeds (optional)

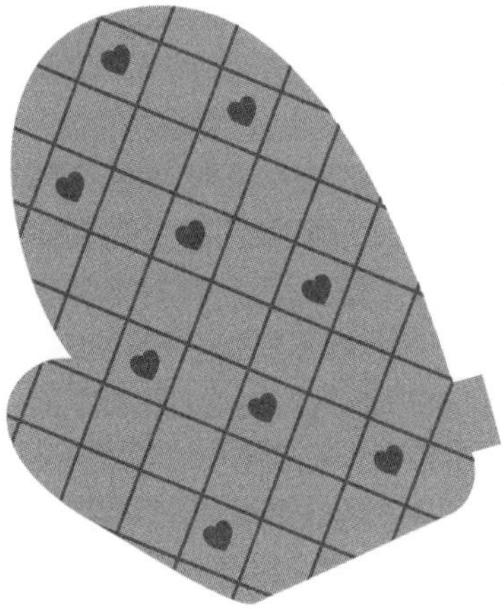

**METHOD**

**1.** Combine the cheese and flour in a bowl, then season with pepper. Gradually work in enough of the egg to mix to a chunky dough that just holds together. Shape into a thick roll about 20cm/8in long, wrap in clingfilm and chill for 30 minutes, or longer if you have time.

**2.** Heat the oven to 180°C/350°F/gas 4 and grease or line a large baking sheet.

**3.** Cut the roll into 5mm/¼in slices and arrange them on the prepared baking sheet. Sprinkle with poppy seeds, if liked.

**4.** Bake in the oven for 10 minutes until brown at the edges.

**5.** Leave to cool on the baking sheet for 1 minute, then transfer to a wire rack to finish cooling.

# Potato Biscuits

✳ ✳ ✳ ✳ ✳ ✳ ✳ ✳

*These are tasty biscuits that go well with cheese.*
*They are a great way to use up any leftover mashed potatoes.*

**INGREDIENTS** *Makes 20 biscuits*

100g/4oz plain flour, plus extra
   for dusting
100g/4oz rolled oats
½ tsp salt
75g/3oz butter
100g/4oz cold mashed potatoes

**MAKE THEM GLUTEN-FREE**
Substitute gluten-free plain
flour to make these biscuits
suitable for most people who
have a gluten intolerance.

**METHOD**

**1.** Heat the oven to 160°C/325°F/
gas 3 and grease or line two
baking sheets.
**2.** Put the flour, oats and salt in
a bowl. Rub in the butter until
the mixture resembles coarse
breadcrumbs. Stir in the mashed
potatoes and mix to a firm dough.
**3.** Roll out on a lightly floured
surface to about 5mm/¼in
thick and cut into rounds with a
7.5cm/3in biscuit cutter. Arrange
on the prepared baking sheet.
**4.** Bake in the oven for 20 minutes
until crisp and brown.
**5.** Leave to cool on the baking
sheet for 1 minute, then transfer to
a wire rack to finish cooling.

# Sesame Snaps

❈ ❈ ❈ ❈ ❈ ❈ ❈

*Tasty little oat biscuits, these can be served with cheese or pâté.*
*The sprinkling of sesame seeds gives extra flavour and crunch,*
*and looks good too.*

## INGREDIENTS *Makes 16 biscuits*

175g/6oz wholemeal flour,
   plus extra for dusting
50g/2oz fine oatmeal
½ tsp cayenne pepper
a pinch of salt
50g/2oz butter
2 tbsp sesame seeds
1 egg, lightly beaten
3–4 tbsp milk
1 tsp caraway seeds

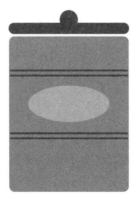

## METHOD

**1.** Heat the oven to 190°C/350°F/
gas 5 and grease or line a large
baking sheet.

**2.** Put the flour, oatmeal, cayenne
pepper and salt in a bowl. Rub
in the butter until the mixture
resembles coarse breadcrumbs.
Stir in the sesame seeds. Add the
egg and enough of the milk to mix
to a firm dough.

**3.** Roll out on a lightly floured
surface to about 5mm/¼in thick and
cut into rounds with a 7.5cm/3in
biscuit cutter. Arrange on the
prepared baking sheet and sprinkle
with the caraway seeds.

**4.** Bake in the oven for 15 minutes
until golden brown.

**5.** Leave to cool on the baking sheet
for 1 minute, then transfer to a wire
rack to finish cooling.

# Plain Rusks

✳ ✳ ✳ ✳ ✳ ✳ ✳ ✳

*This traditional recipe is for crackers to serve with savoury accompaniments such as cheese or pâté. They are twice-baked to make them really crisp.*

**INGREDIENTS** *Makes 18 rusks*
225g/8oz self-raising flour, plus
    extra for dusting
a pinch of salt
75g/3oz butter
1 egg, lightly beaten
3–4 tbsp milk

**METHOD**
**1.** Heat the oven to 220°C/425°F/
gas 7 and grease or line two
baking sheets.
**2.** Put the flour and salt in a bowl.
Rub in the butter until the mixture
resembles coarse breadcrumbs.
Add the egg, then just enough of

the milk to mix to a firm dough.
**3.** Roll out on a lightly floured
surface to about 2.5mm/1in thick
and cut into rounds with a 7.5cm/3in
biscuit cutter. Arrange on the
prepared baking sheets.
**4.** Bake for 10 minutes, then remove
from the oven and reduce the
temperature to 190°C/375°F/gas 5.
**5.** Split the rusks in half horizontally.
Place back on the baking sheets,
cut-side up, and bake for 15 minutes
until really crisp and golden brown.
**6.** Leave to cool on the baking sheet
for 1 minute, then transfer to a wire
rack to finish cooling.

# Barbadian Conkies

❄ ❄ ❄ ❄ ❄ ❄ ❄

*These are a great way of using up the pumpkin flesh scraped out of Halloween pumpkin lanterns. If you want to make them at a time when fresh pumpkin isn't available, use canned.*

**INGREDIENTS** *Makes 12 conkies*
350g/12oz pumpkin flesh, grated
225g/8oz sweet potato, peeled
   and grated
225g/8oz desiccated coconut
350g/12oz dark brown soft sugar
1 tsp mixed spice
1 tsp freshly grated nutmeg
a pinch of salt
1 tsp almond extract
350g/12oz cornmeal
100g/4oz self-raising flour
100g/4oz raisins
175g/6oz butter, melted
300m/10fl oz milk

**METHOD**
**1.** Set up a steamer, if you have one, or put a heatproof bowl on top of a saucepan half-filled with boiling water with the saucepan lid on top. Cut twelve 20cm/8in squares of kitchen foil.

**2.** Put the pumpkin, sweet potato, coconut, sugar, spices, salt and almond extract in a bowl and mix together. Gradually work in the cornmeal, flour and raisins. Add the melted butter and milk and blend to combine.
**3.** Shape the mixture into 12 balls and divide among the foil squares. Fold each one into a parcel, twisting to seal the top. Place the parcels in the steamer or the bowl, cover, and steam for about 1 hour until firm. Serve hot or cold.

**FRESH COCONUT**
For authenticity, you can use the flesh of 1 large coconut, grated, instead of desiccated coconut, as is done in Barbados.

# CHAPTER 8

✳✳✳✳✳✳✳✳

# GLUTEN-FREE BISCUITS

There are now some gluten-free biscuits available in the shops, but if you make your own, you will enjoy a much wider variety.

# Keeping it gluten-free

✽ ✽ ✽ ✽ ✽ ✽ ✽ ✽

If you believe you may be gluten-intolerant you should consult your doctor for advice before changing your diet. However, in this chapter there are some recipes you are sure to enjoy whether or not you have a problem with gluten.

If gluten-free cooking is new to you, go through your food cupboard and read the labels. This way you will be much more likely to remember where to look for gluten in products when you are shopping and what you need to avoid. Here are a few things to look out for – but this is not an exhaustive list.

* Wheat flours of all kinds and anything made with them, so bread, cakes, pasta, and cereals.
* Any wheat products such as wheatgerm, semolina, couscous or bran.
* Any products containing rye, barley, spelt, and kamut. Some people also cannot tolerate oats, which contain a protein similar to gluten and may have been milled in equipment used for wheat, rye and barley.
* Raising agents such as baking powder or bicarbonate of soda.
* Spices, which sometimes use flour to stop them clumping.
* Sauces, condiments or anything that is thickened with wheat flour.

Don't dwell on what you can't eat – be imaginative and find things you can, and ways of adapting your favourite recipes.

Special gluten-free flours, baking powder and other products are readily available. For biscuits, you don't usually need xanthan gum, but I have included it in one or two cake-like recipes as it restores the springy texture that you lose when you bake without gluten. Use nuts in your cooking, finely ground. Try other grains and grain products, such as cornflour, buckwheat, and rice flour.

# Gluten-free Tea Biscuits

❋ ❋ ❋ ❋ ❋ ❋ ❋ ❋

*These are simple little biscuits to accompany the first cup of tea of the morning; they work well with gluten-free flour.*

**INGREDIENTS** *Makes 12 biscuits*
250g/9oz gluten-free plain flour
1 tsp gluten-free baking powder
¼ tsp xanthan gum
a pinch of salt
60g/2½oz vegetable fat
1 egg, lightly beaten
150ml/5fl oz milk

**METHOD**
**1.** Heat the oven to 200°C/400°F/ gas 6 and grease or line a large baking sheet.
**2.** Put the flour, baking powder, xanthan gum and salt in a bowl and rub in the fat until the mixture resembles coarse breadcrumbs. Add the egg and enough of the milk to mix to a soft dough.
**3.** Roll out on a lightly floured surface to about 5mm/¼in thick and cut into 7.5cm/3in rounds with a smooth biscuit cutter. Arrange on the prepared baking sheet.
**4.** Bake in the oven for about 12 minutes until golden brown.
**5.** Leave to cool on the baking sheet for 1 minute, then transfer to a wire rack to finish cooling.

# Gluten-free Shortbread

✳ ✳ ✳ ✳ ✳ ✳ ✳ ✳

*Just sugar, butter and flour, shortbread is one of the simplest and most classic biscuits and you'll get good results with this mix of flours. You can make it round and cut it into wedges, or square and cut it into bars.*

**INGREDIENTS** *Makes 8 wedges*
130g/4¾oz butter, softened
50g/2oz caster sugar
50g/2oz cornflour
50g/2oz gram flour
150g/5oz gluten-free plain flour

**METHOD**

**1.** Heat the oven to 160°C/325°F/ gas 3 and grease and line a 20cm/8in cake tin.

**2.** Beat the butter until it is very soft, then work in the sugar, followed by the flours. Start with a wooden spoon, then use your hands.

**3.** Press the mixture into the prepared tin. Prick all over with a fork and cut into eight wedges.

**4.** Bake in the oven for 35 minutes until a pale golden colour.

**5.** Leave to cool in the tin for 2 minutes, then cut through the markings into wedges. Leave to cool for another few minutes before lifting on to a wire rack to finish cooling.

> **ALMOND SHORTBREAD**
> You can also try the recipe on page 81, made with ground almonds, butter and sugar.

# Gluten-free Coconut Biscuits

❋ ❋ ❋ ❋ ❋ ❋ ❋ ❋

*This recipe makes lovely biscuits that all the family will enjoy. Use caster or light brown soft sugar instead of dark brown, if you prefer.*

**INGREDIENTS** *Makes 12 biscuits*

50g/2oz butter, softened
50g/2oz dark brown soft sugar
50g/2oz caster sugar
1 egg, lightly beaten
1 tsp vanilla extract
1 tbsp potato flour, plus extra
  for dusting
25g/1oz rice flour
2 tsp baking powder
1 tsp bicarbonate of soda
25g/1oz desiccated coconut
2 tbsp coconut milk

**METHOD**

**1.** Heat the oven to 200°C/400°F/ gas 6 and grease or line two baking sheets.

**2.** Beat together the butter and sugars until smooth and creamy. Gradually work in the egg and vanilla alternately with spoonfuls of the flours, the baking powder and bicarbonate of soda. Stir in the coconut and coconut milk and mix to a soft dough.

**3.** Shape into small balls with lightly floured hands, flatten slightly, and arrange well apart on the prepared baking sheets.

**4.** Bake in the oven for about 10 minutes until golden brown.

**5.** Leave to cool on the baking sheet for 1 minute, then transfer to a wire rack to finish cooling.

# Gluten-free Choc Chip Cookies

✳ ✳ ✳ ✳ ✳ ✳ ✳ ✳

*No-one should have to go without a chocolate cookie now and then. These are made with whisked egg white so have quite a light, crunchy texture, rather different from a normal chocolate chip cookie.*

**INGREDIENTS** *Makes 18 cookies*

350g/12oz icing sugar, sifted
75g/3oz cocoa powder
a pinch of salt
75g/3oz dark chocolate, chopped
   into chunks
75g/3oz pecan nuts, chopped
1 tbsp sunflower oil
2 eggs, separated

**METHOD**

**1.** Heat the oven to 180°C/350°F/ gas 4 and grease and line two baking sheets.

**2.** Put the sugar, cocoa and salt in a bowl and mix together. Stir in the chocolate and pecans, then the oil and egg yolks.

**3.** In a separate bowl, whisk the egg whites until they form soft peaks, then gently fold them into the cookie mixture with a large metal spoon, stirring as little as possible so you keep as much air in the mixture as you can. Place spoonfuls of the mixture well apart on the prepared baking sheets.

**4.** Bake in the oven for 20 minutes until the cookies have spread and the tops are cracked and dry.

**5.** Leave to cool on the baking sheet for 5 minutes, then transfer to a wire rack to finish cooling. Do not attempt to move them until they have cooled and hardened otherwise they will crumble into bits.

# Gluten-free Hazelnut & Treacle Cookies

✳ ✳ ✳ ✳ ✳ ✳ ✳ ✳

*These are rugged and crunchy biscuits, great for the lunch box.
Use other nuts of your choice if you don't have hazelnuts.*

**INGREDIENTS** *Makes 12 cookies*

100g/4oz black treacle
100g/4oz butter
100g/4oz dark brown soft sugar
100g/4oz ground hazelnuts
100g/4oz cornflour
a pinch of salt
1 egg, lightly beaten

**METHOD**

**1.** Heat the oven to 190°C/375°F/ gas 5 and grease or line a large baking sheet.
**2.** Gently melt the treacle, butter and sugar in a pan, stirring together. Stir in the hazelnuts, cornflour, salt and egg and mix to a smooth dough.
**3.** Roll into balls about the size of a walnut and press them slightly flat. Arrange on the baking sheet.

**4.** Bake in the oven for about 20 minutes until golden brown.
**5.** Leave to cool on the baking sheets for 1 minute, then transfer to a wire rack to finish cooling.

# Gluten-free Butter & Maple Syrup Creams

✳ ✳ ✳ ✳ ✳ ✳ ✳

*Soft and melting biscuits sandwiched with a
maple syrup-flavoured buttercream, these are delicious.
Use honey instead of maple syrup if you prefer.*

## INGREDIENTS *Makes 12 biscuits*

150g/5oz butter
50g/2oz golden syrup
2 tbsp maple syrup
100g/4oz cornflour
100g/4oz gluten-free plain flour
50g/2oz rice flour
1 egg, lightly beaten
1 tsp vanilla extract

### FOR THE FILLING

30g/1oz butter
1 tsp maple syrup
45g/1¾oz icing sugar, sifted

## METHOD

**1.** Heat the oven to 200°C/400°F/
gas 6 and grease and line two
baking sheets.
**2.** Put the butter, syrup and maple
syrup in a bowl and beat until
smooth and creamy. Gradually
work in the flours, egg and vanilla
and mix to a soft dough. Place
24 spoonfuls well apart on the
prepared baking sheets.
**3.** Bake in the oven for 15 minutes
until golden brown.
**4.** Leave to cool on the baking sheets
for 1 minute, then transfer to a wire
rack to finish cooling.
**5.** Beat the filling ingredients together
until smooth, then use to sandwich
the biscuits together in pairs.

# Gluten-free Spiced Sesame biscuits

*You can make these a little hotter with more cayenne, if you like, but 1 tsp gives quite a spicy biscuit. Yellow cornmeal can be substituted for white maize meal.*

**INGREDIENTS** *Makes 16 biscuits*

175g/6oz white maize meal
25g/1oz cornflour, plus extra for dusting
50g/2oz gram flour
½–1 tsp cayenne pepper
salt and freshly ground black pepper
50g/2oz butter
1 egg, lightly beaten
3–4 tbsp milk
2 tbsp sesame seeds

**METHOD**

**1.** Heat the oven to 190°C/350°F/gas 5 and grease or line a large baking sheet.

**2.** Put the flours, cayenne and salt and pepper in a bowl. Rub in the butter until the mixture resembles coarse breadcrumbs. Add the egg and enough milk to mix to a firm dough.

**3.** Roll out on a lightly floured surface to about 5mm/¼in thick and cut into squares with a 7.5cm/3in biscuit cutter. Arrange on the prepared baking sheet, brush with a little milk and sprinkle with the sesame seeds.

**4.** Bake in the oven for 15 minutes until golden brown.

**5.** Leave to cool on the baking sheet for 1 minute, then transfer to a wire rack to finish cooling.

# Gluten-free Crisp Parmesan Crackers

✳ ✳ ✳ ✳ ✳ ✳ ✳ ✳

*These tasty, cheesy biscuits are slightly crumbly, so they are best with soft dips rather than anything that is more unyielding.*

**INGREDIENTS** *Makes 12 biscuits*

100g/4oz gram flour
50g/2oz gluten-free plain flour,
  plus extra for dusting
50g/2oz Parmesan cheese,
  freshly grated
½ tsp gluten-free baking powder
salt and freshly ground black pepper
4 tbsp olive oil
3–4 tbsp boiling water

**METHOD**

**1.** Heat the oven to 190°C/350°F/ gas 5 and grease or line a large baking sheet.

**2.** Put the flours, cheese and baking powder in a bowl and season with a little salt and plenty of pepper. Stir in the oil and enough boiling water to mix to a rather crumbly dough.

**3.** Roll out on a lightly floured surface to about 5mm/¼in thick and cut into squares. Arrange on the prepared baking sheet.

**4.** Bake in the oven for 15 minutes until golden brown.

**5.** Leave to cool on the baking sheet for about 1 minute, then transfer to a wire rack to finish cooling.

# Gluten-free Oat Biscuits

✳ ✳ ✳ ✳ ✳ ✳ ✳ ✳

*It's surprising how many commercially made oat biscuits also contain wheat, so it's safest to make your own – and these are delicious.*

**INGREDIENTS** *Makes 12 biscuits*
100g/4oz medium oatmeal
40g/1½oz oat flour, plus extra
   for dusting
½ tsp gluten-free baking powder
25g/1oz butter
1–2 tsp boiling water

**METHOD**
**1.** Heat the oven to 190°C/350°F/
gas 5 and grease or line a large
baking sheet.
**2.** Put the oatmeal, flour and baking powder in a bowl. Rub in the butter until the mixture resembles coarse breadcrumbs. Stir in enough of the boiling water to mix to a soft dough.
**3.** Roll out on a lightly floured surface to about 5mm/¼in thick and cut into squares or fingers. Arrange on the prepared baking sheet.
**4.** Bake in the oven for 15 minutes until golden brown.
**5.** Leave to cool on the baking sheet for about 1 minute, then transfer to a wire rack to finish cooling.

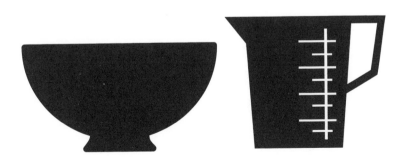

# Index

✳ ✳ ✳ ✳ ✳ ✳ ✳